1000

1000 JEWELRY
INSPIRATIONS

QUARRY

1000 JEWELRY INSPIRATIONS

BEADS, BAUBLES, DANGLES, AND CHAINS

SANDRA SALAMONY

BEVERLY MASSACHUSETTS

QUARRY BOOKS

First published in the United States of America by
Quarry Books, a member of
Quayside Publishing Group
100 Cummings Center
Suite 406-L
Beverly, Massachusetts 01915-6101
Telephone: (978) 282-9590
Fax: (978) 283-2742
www.quarrybooks.com

Library of Congress Cataloging-in-Publication Data
Salamony, Sandra.
  1,000 jewelry inspirations : beads, baubles, dangles, and chains / Sandra Salamony.
    p. cm.
  Includes index.
  ISBN 1-59253-413-9
  1. Jewelry making. I. Title. II. Title: One thousand jewelry inspirations.
  TT212.S24 2008
  739.27--dc22

                                    2007042955

ISBN-13: 978-1-59253-413-5
ISBN-10: 1-59253-413-9

10 9 8 7 6 5 4 3 2

Cover and interior design: Sandra Salamony
Material on pages 302-311 adapted from *Making Designer Bead and Wire Jewelry* (Quarry Books, 2005)
Illustrations: Judy Love

Printed in China

Dedicated to the hundreds of artists
who contributed to this book.
They've inspired me, and I hope they'll inspire you, too.

contents

introduction

What makes a piece of jewelry special?

When creating handmade jewelry, a personalization of the piece is what separates it from the ordinary: incorporating a vintage bead, a found object, a much-loved image, or even a scrap from a recycled sweater or favorite fabric. Sometimes, it's developing an unusual technique or designing around a vibrant use of color, texture, or contrast that makes the jewelry unique. Unlike purchasing a mass-produced piece of jewelry, creating an original piece by hand is truly creating wearable art.

This book showcases a stunning collection of original jewelry created by artists from all over the world. Chosen for their creative details or their overall aesthetic, these pieces feature techniques such as collage, wirework, lampwork, and weaving; materials such as paper, fabric, wire, beads, clay, and paint; and

styles ranging from classic to dramatic. Some pieces are breathtaking in their simplicity, others are delightful in their elaborate layers of color and media. And, amazingly, while most of the artists in each section started with similar raw materials, their results are beautifully varied.

Explore the pages at leisure, and let the artists' creativity inspire your next project. Perhaps an unusual color combination will catch your eye, or you'll be tempted to try a new technique. This book is a gallery of inspirations and also includes a guide to basic jewelry-making techniques to help you get started. Expand your skills and reflect your personality by incorporating new ideas and whimsy into your homemade jewelry. Enjoy!

beads + baubles

0001 KINCAIDESIGNS

0002 McFARLAND DESIGNS

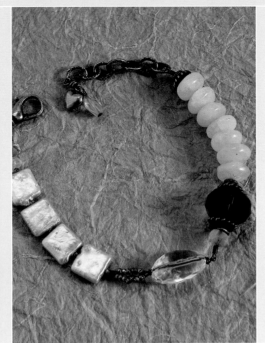

0003 MARY L. SOISSON,
WWW.BELLEDESIGNS.NET

0004 NICOLE NOELLE

0005 NICOLE NOELLE

0006 KELLIOPE

0007 MODERNJEWELRYART.COM

0008 HELOISE

0009 CAROL A. BABINEAU, ART CLAY STUDIO
LAMPWORK BEADS BY LILIANA GLENN

0010 GIRLIE GIRLS JEWELRY STUDIO

0011 SHARON MUTTOO

0012 McFARLAND DESIGNS

0013 PAPER FLOWER GIRL

0014 BEAD JEWELRY BY SHOPGIRL

0015 BEAD JEWELRY BY SHOPGIRL

0016 BEAD JEWELRY BY SHOPGIRL

0017 BEAD JEWELRY BY SHOPGIRL
LAMPWORK BEADS BY LINDA JAMES

0018 KIARA M. McNULTY

0019 KATHLEEN MALEY

0020 KELLIOPE

0021 GIRLIE GIRLS JEWELRY STUDIO

0022 KELLIOPE

0023 KIARA M. McNULTY

0024   SUSAN KUSLANSKY, GODSAGA JEWELRY

0025 TERRY L. CARTER

0026 AMY BOLING

0027 SHARI BONNIN

0028 CHERI AUERBACH

0029 SHARI BONNIN

0030 TAMMY POWLEY

0031 PAPER FLOWER GIRL

0032 TAMMY POWLEY

0033 TAMMY POWLEY

0034 BEAD JEWELRY BY SHOPGIRL

0035 MICHELLE LAMBERT

0036 BEAD JEWELRY BY SHOPGIRL
DESIGN CONCEPT BY JILL GANDOLFINI; LAMPWORK BEAD BY LINDA JAMES

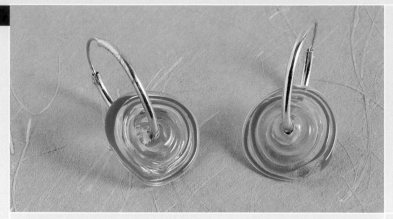

0037 JENNIFER SYFU

0038 MARIE F. FIEDRICH, CERCA TROVA

0039 PHAEDRA A. TORRES, LLUVIA DESIGNS

0040 RICKIE VOGES DESIGN
LAMPWORK BY MELANIE MOERTEL, MELANIE.MOERTEL GLASPERLEN

0041 MIA GOFAR JEWELRY

0042 KIARA M. McNULTY

0043 JENNIFER SHIBONA

0044 PHAEDRA A. TORRES, LLUVIA DESIGNS

0045 RICKIE VOGES DESIGN
LAMPWORK BY DAWN WHITE, DUDA DESIGNS

0046 WANDRDESIGN BY WENDY

0047 MICALLA JEWELRY AND DESIGNS, CAMILLA JØRGENSEN
PHOTO BY CARLOS DAVILA

0048 DIANA SAMPER

0049 STONZ

0050 STONZ

0051 MELANI WILSON DESIGNS

0052 DIANA SAMPER

0053 STONZ

0054 MANDALA JEWELS
MANDALAJEWELS.ETSY.COM

0055 LISA LAMPE

0056 TAMMY POWLEY

0057 THERESA MINK DESIGNS

0058 CYNDI LAVIN

0059 JADES CREATIONS
HANDCRAFTED JEWELRY

0060 LISA LAMPE

0061 McFARLAND DESIGNS

0062 RICKIE VOGES DESIGN
LAMPWORK BY CARRIE BERRY, HARDWOOD TRAIL GLASS

0063 THERESA MINK DESIGNS

0064 RHONA FARBER
OVERTHEMOONJEWELRY.COM

0065 PEGGY PRIELOZNY

0066 TAMMY POWLEY

0067   KAY LANCASHIRE, KAY'S ARTYCLES

0068 RICKIE VOGES DESIGN
LAMPWORK BY KIMBERLY LYNN, KIMBEADS

0069 SHERRI FORRESTER

0070 LISA LAMPE

0071 TRACEY H. THOMASSON

0072 KAY LANCASHIRE, KAY'S ARTYCLES

0073 MOOD SWING

0074 NATALIE MAGARIAN, PASHUPATINA

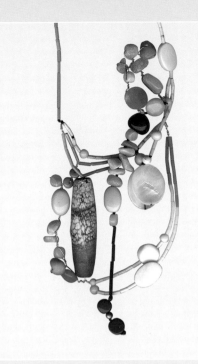

0075 NATALIE MAGARIAN, PASHUPATINA

0076 NATALIE MAGARIAN, PASHUPATINA

0077 NATALIE MAGARIAN, PASHUPATINA

0078 NATALIE MAGARIAN, PASHUPATINA

0079 NATALIE MAGARIAN, PASHUPATINA

0080 JENNIFER SYFU

0081 McFARLAND DESIGNS

0082 McFARLAND DESIGNS

0083 AMY BOLING

0084 AMY BOLING

0085 LILI HALL, ARTEFACT

0086 McFARLAND DESIGNS

0088 MANDALA JEWELS
MANDALAJEWELS.ETSY.COM

0089 MANDALA JEWELS
MANDALAJEWELS.ETSY.COM

0090 MANDALA JEWELS
MANDALAJEWELS.ETSY.COM

0091 MANDALA JEWELS
MANDALAJEWELS.ETSY.COM

0092 CYNDI LAVIN

0093 NICHOLE HILTS, BEVERLYBIJOU

0094 KATHLEEN MALEY

0095 SALLY NUNNALLY

0096 AGNES ARUCAN

0097 AGNES ARUCAN

0098 KINCAIDESIGNS

0099 MARIE F. FIEDRICH, CERCA TROVA
ROUND GLASS BEADS BY MELISSA PERRY McQUILKIN/WHITNEY STREET STUDIO
RECTANGLE BEADS BY ANGELA BERNARD/GENERATIONS LAMPWORKBEADS

0100 YAEL MILLER DESIGN

0101 SARAH GORDEN, SOJOURN CURIOSITIES

0102 RANDI SAMUELS

0103   CYNDI LAVIN

0104 KINCAIDESIGN

0105   BEAD JEWELRY BY SHOPGIRL

0106   BEAD JEWELRY BY SHOPGIRL

0107   LILLIE WOLFF DESIGNS

0108   KIARA M. McNULTY

0109   AGNES ARUCAN

0110   McFARLAND DESIGNS

0111   BEAD JEWELRY BY SHOPGIRL

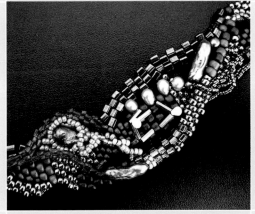

0112   BEAD JEWELRY BY SHOPGIRL

0113   BEAD JEWELRY BY SHOPGIRL

0114   JENNI PAGANO

0115   LILLIE WOLFF DESIGNS

0116   ERIN SARGEANT, LIKE A FOX

0117   BEAD JEWELRY BY SHOPGIRL

0118   TAMMY POWLEY

0119   MANDALA JEWELS
MANDALAJEWELS.ETSY.COM

0120 PHAEDRA A. TORRES, LLUVIA DESIGNS

0121   KIARA M. McNULTY

0122   RICKIE VOGES DESIGN
LAMPWORK BY KIMBERY LYNN, KIMBEADS

0123   BEAD JEWELRY BY SHOPGIRL

0124   NICOLE NOELLE

0125 NICOLE NOELLE

0126 JENNI PAGANO

0127 MICALLA JEWELRY AND DESIGNS, CAMILLA JØRGENSEN
PHOTO BY CARLOS DAVILA

0128 McFARLAND DESIGNS

0129 MARIE F. FIEDRICH, CERCA TROVA
FOCAL BEAD MADE BY BERNADETTE FUENTES; SEA GLASS BEADS BY ANGELA "GELLY" DAVIS

0130 MONA SONG DESIGNS

0131 KATHLEEN MALEY

0132 MARIE F. FIEDRICH, CERCA TROVA
LAMPWORK BEADS BY CHET CORNELIUSON/BCLAMPWORK

0133 MARIE F. FIEDRICH, CERCA TROVA
LAMPWORK BEADS BY ANGELA "GELLY" DAVIS

0134 BEAD JEWELRY BY SHOPGIRL

0135 BEAD JEWELRY BY SHOPGIRL

0136 JANET BASKERVILLE, JBASK ARTS
PHOTO BY MICHAEL J. JOYCE

0137 KIARA M. McNULTY

0138 BELLE POUR LA VIE, BELLEPOURLAVIE.COM

0139 RENEE THOMAS
LAMPWORK BEADS BY HEATHER DAVIS. SCULPTED ROSES BY D. JEAN VAINIO

0140 TAMMY POWLEY

0141 BELLE POUR LA VIE,
BELLEPOURLAVIE.COM

0142 JENNI PAGANO

0143 CHERI AUERBACH

0144 MANDALA JEWELS
MANDALAJEWELS.ETSY.COM

0145 BEAD JEWELRY BY SHOPGIRL

0146 RICKIE VOGES DESIGN
LAMPWORK BY JENA FULCHER, JENAGIRL BEADS

0147 PHAEDRA A. TORRES, LLUVIA DESIGNS

0148 GIRLIE GIRLS JEWELRY STUDIO

0149 GIRLIE GIRLS JEWELRY STUDIO

0150 STUDIO47WEST

0151 KIARA M. McNULTY

0152 CHERI AUERBACH

0153 LINDSAY STREEM

0154 McFARLAND DESIGNS

0155 SARAH GORDEN,
SOJOURN CURIOSITIES

0156 JENNI PAGANO

0157 KIARA M. McNULTY

0158 HELOISE

0159 McFARLAND DESIGNS

0160 PAPER FLOWER GIRL

0161 MANDALA JEWELS, MANDALAJEWELS.ETSY.COM

0162 DEBORAH FRANKS,
ARTWORKS.ETSY.COM

0163 STUDIO47WEST

0164 TAMMY POWLEY

0165 TAMMY POWLEY

0166 LISA LAMPE

0167 NICOLE NOELLE

0168 TAMMY POWLEY

0169 MIA GOFAR JEWELRY

0170 BEAD JEWELRY BY SHOPGIRL

0171 YAEL MILLER DESIGN

0172 JQ JEWELRY DESIGNS

0173 MIA GOFAR JEWELRY

0174 BEAD JEWELRY BY SHOPGIRL

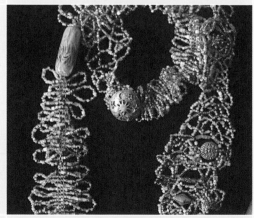

0175 JANET BASKERVILLE, JBASK ARTS
PHOTO BY MICHAEL J. JOYCE

0176 CHERI AUERBACH

0177 TAMMY POWLEY

0178 AGNES ARUCAN

0179 PAPER FLOWER GIRL

0180 BELLE POUR LA VIE,
BELLEPOURLAVIE.COM

0181 JQ JEWELRY DESIGNS

0182 JQ JEWELRY DESIGNS

0183 SUSAN D. WIMBLEY

0184 SARAH GORDEN,
SOJOURN CURIOSITIES

0185 MARY L. SOISSON
BELLEDESIGNS.NET

0186 MOOD SWING

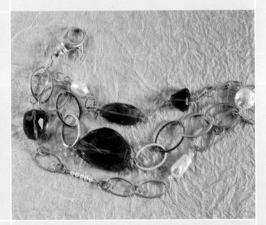

0187 MELANI WILSON DESIGNS

0188   JENNIFER SYFU

0189   PHAEDRA A. TORRES,
LLUVIA DESIGNS

0190   SARAH GORDEN,
SOJOURN CURIOSITIES

0191   SARAH GORDEN,
SOJOURN CURIOSITIES

0192   ROCCA DESIGNS,
CAROLINA ESTRADA

0193   JANET BASKERVILLE, JBASK ARTS
PHOTO BY MICHAEL J. JOYCE

0194 AGNES ARUCAN

0195   AGNES ARUCAN

0196 ERIN SARGEANT

0197 THERESA MINK DESIGNS

0198 MONA SONG DESIGNS

0199 WANDRWEDDING BY WENDY

0200 SARAH GORDEN,
SOJOURN CURIOSITIES

0201 KELLIOPE

0202 SARAH GORDEN,
SOJOURN CURIOSITIES

0203 MARIE F. FIEDRICH, CERCA TROVA
BEADS BY ANGELA "GELLY" DAVIS

0204 SUSAN D. WIMBLEY

0205 GIRLY GIRLS JEWELRY STUDIO

0206 JADES CREATIONS
HANDCRAFTED JEWELRY

0207 MICALLA JEWELRY AND DESIGNS,
CAMILLA JØRGENSEN
PHOTO BY CARLOS DAVILA

0208   DEBORAH FRANKS, ARTWORKS.ETSY.COM

0209　KIONA WILSON, LUCKY ACCESSORIES

0210 PRECIOUS MESHES, EMILY CONROY

0211 KAY DANIELS, KAY DESIGNS

0212 JADES CREATIONS
HANDCRAFTED JEWELRY

0213 KIARA M. McNULTY

0214 SALLY NUNNALLY

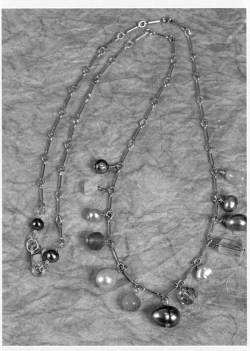

0215 RHONA FARBER

0216 MARIE F. FIEDRICH, CERCA TROVA

0217 ERIN SARGEANT, LIKE A FOX

0218 TAMMY POWLEY

0219 BEAD JEWELRY BY SHOPGIRL

0221   SUZANNE L. HELWIG

0222 TAMMY POWLEY

0223 TAMMY POWLEY

0224 PAM KARABINOS,
MYSMYRRH DESIGNS
PHOTO BY STEPHANIE BRIGGS, BRIGGS PHOTOGRAPHY

0225 TAMMY POWLEY

0226 TAMMY POWLEY

0227 TAMMY POWLEY

0228 TAMMY POWLEY

0229 RUBY FISCHER

0230 KATE FERRANT

0231 CYNDY KLEIN

0232 HEATHER MANN

0233 BELLE POUR LA VIE, BELLEPOURLAVIE.COM

0234 DAWN M. LOMBARD. LAVENDER DAWN

0235   KIONA WILSON, LUCKY ACCESSORIES

0236 DAPHNE "D.D." HESS

0237 JOANNE STREHLE BAST

0238 TAMMY POWLEY

0239 CHERI AUERBACH

0240 JOANNE STREHLE BAST

0241 TAMMY POWLEY

0242 RICKIE VOGES DESIGN
LAMPWORK BY ANDREA VENSCHOTT,
ANNAKALILLY'S HANDGERABEITETE GLASPERLEN

0243 SHIHO YAMASHITA

0244 TAMMY POWLEY

0245 TAMMY POWLEY

0246 McFARLAND DESIGNS

0247 **MICALLA JEWELRY AND DESIGNS, CAMILLA JØRGENSEN**
PHOTO BY CARLOS DAVILA

0248 **JANICE PARSONS**

0249 **MONA SONG DESIGNS**

0250 **DAWN CECCACCI**

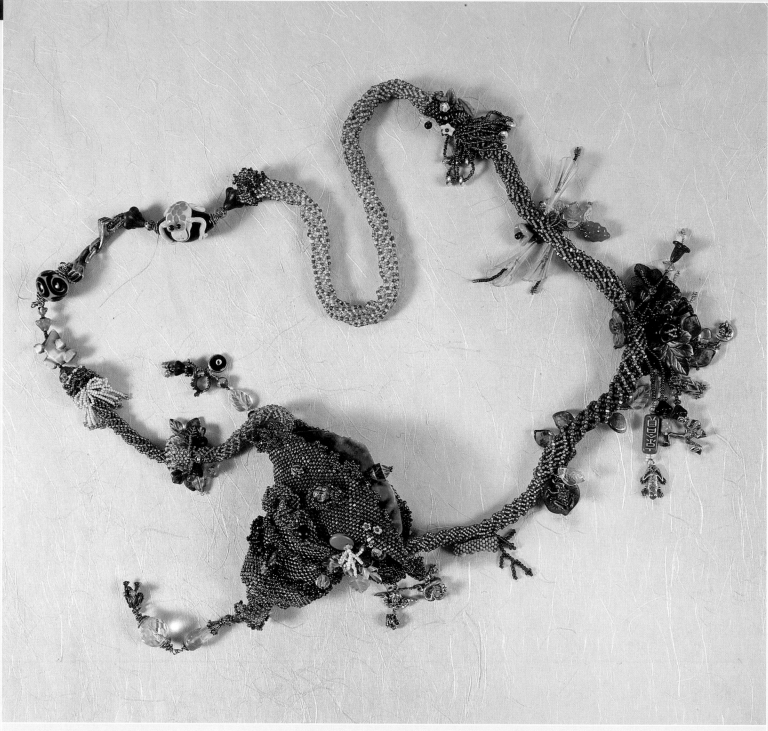

0251 MARCIA ACKER-MISSALL

0252 DANA LYNN DRISCOLL

0253 TAMMY POWLEY

0254 BRENDA HOFFMAN

0255 ROCCA DESIGNS, CAROLINA ESTRADA

0256 JENNIFER SYFU

0257 SALLY NUNNALLY

0258 SARAH J. BABINEAU

0259 TAMMY POWLEY

0260 LISA NIVEN KELLY

0261 JENNIFER SYFU

0262 KINCAIDESIGNS

0263 TAMMY POWLEY

0264 MARCIA ACKER-MISSALL

0265 **RICKIE VOGES DESIGN**
LAMPWORK BY MELANIE MOERTEL, MELANIE.MOERTEL GLASPERLEN

0266 **THERESA MINK DESIGNS**

0267 LISA LAMPE

0268 NICOLE NOELLE

0269 NICOLE NOELLE

0270 NICOLE NOELLE

0271 STUDIO47WEST

0272 NICOLE NOELLE

0273 NICOLE NOELLE

0274 McFARLAND DESIGNS

0275 NICOLE NOELLE

0276 SHIHO YAMASHITA

0277 STUDIO47WEST

0278 TAMMY POWLEY

0279 DAWN M. LOMBARD, LAVENDER DAWN

0280 DANA LYNN DRISCOLL

0281 MANDALA JEWELS, MANDALAJEWELS.ETSY.COM

0282 MICALLA JEWELRY AND DESIGNS, CAMILLA JØRGENSEN
PHOTO BY CARLOS DAVILA

0283 CHERI AUERBACH

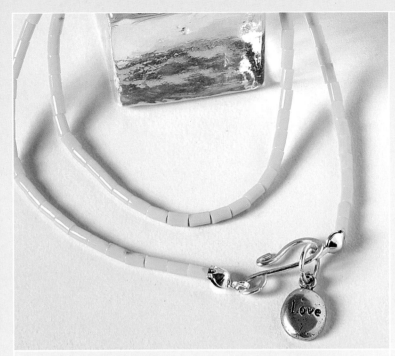

0284 TAMMY POWLEY

0285 TAMMY POWLEY

0286 JESSICA NEAVES

0287 PAPER FLOWER GIRL

0288 NICOLE NOELLE

0289 NICOLE NOELLE

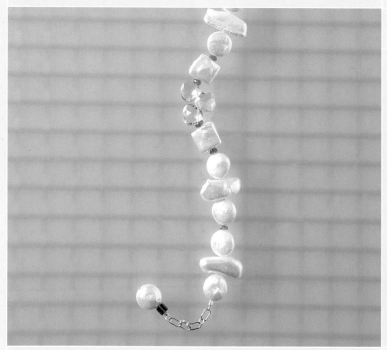

0290 NICOLE NOELLE

0291 NICOLE NOELLE

0292   NICOLE NOELLE

0293 RELISHDRESS

0294 HALLE GUSTAFSON

0295 MOOD SWING

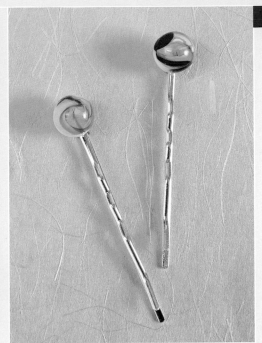

0296 JENNIFER SYFU

0297 NICOLE NOELLE

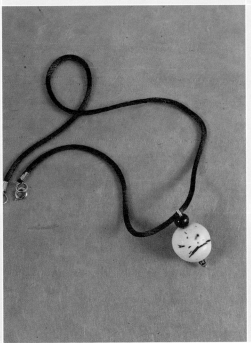

0298 DIANA SAMPER

0299 DAWN BARKER, HARDFLOWER STUDIOS

0300 GIRLIE GIRLS JEWELRY STUDIO

0301 DIANA SAMPER

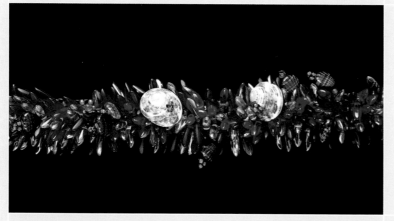

0302 KIARA M. McNULTY

0303 MARCIA ACKER-MISSALL

0304 STEPHANIE RIGER JEWELRY, STEPHANIERIGER.COM

0305 MARIE F. FIEDRICH, CERCA TROVA

0306 DAWN M. LOMBARD, LAVENDER DAWN

0307   MANDALA JEWELS, MANDALAJEWELS.ETSY.COM

0308 RHONA FARBER
OVERTHEMOONJEWELRY.COM

0309 NICOLE NOELLE

0310 BRUNA VASCONCELOS

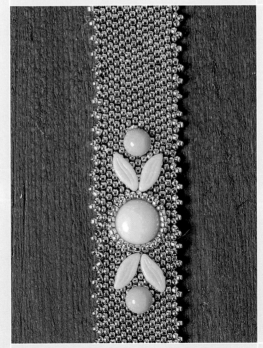

0311 RUBY FISCHER

0312 NICOLE NOELLE

0313 MONA SONG DESIGNS

paper + mixed media

chapter 2

0314–0440

0314 ELIZABETH GLASS GELTMAN + RACHEL GELTMAN

0315 AMY HELM

0316 MAGGIE KRAWCZYK, NEOGAMI ORGANIC JEWELRY, NEOGAMI.COM

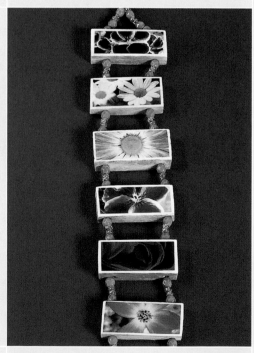

0317 JANET BASKERVILLE, JBASK ARTS
PHOTO BY MICHAEL J. JOYCE

0318 ELIZABETH GLASS GELTMAN + RACHEL GELTMAN

0319 ANN WIDNER

0320 VICKIE ZUMPF

0321 SANDRA TATSUKO KADOWAKI

0322 MODERNJEWELRYART.COM

0323 NANCY ANDERSON,
SWEET BIRD STUDIO

0324 HELOISE

0325 SANDRA TATSUKO KADOWAKI

0326 ANA PEREIRA

0327 TAMMY POWLEY

0328 NANCY ANDERSON, SWEET BIRD STUDIO

0329 NANCY ANDERSON, SWEET BIRD STUDIO

0330 NANCY ANDERSON, SWEET BIRD STUDIO

0331 NANCY ANDERSON, SWEET BIRD STUDIO

0332 NANCY ANDERSON, SWEET BIRD STUDIO

0333 IVORY EILEEN, PAPER ORGANICS JEWELRY

0334 IVORY EILEEN, PAPER ORGANICS JEWELRY

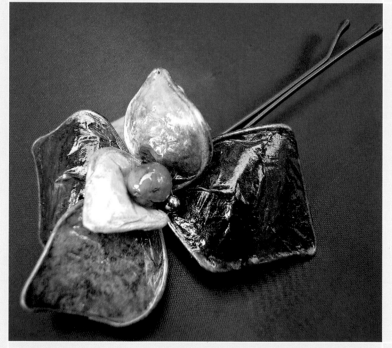

0335 IVORY EILEEN, PAPER ORGANICS JEWELRY

0336 IVORY EILEEN, PAPER ORGANICS JEWELRY

0337 IVORY EILEEN, PAPER ORGANICS JEWELRY

0338 **HALLIGAN NORRIS**
PHOTO BY JOSH GOLEMAN

0339 **HALLIGAN NORRIS**
PHOTO BY JOSH GOLEMAN

0340 **HALLIGAN NORRIS**
PHOTO BY JOSH GOLEMAN

0341 **HALLIGAN NORRIS**
PHOTO BY JOSH GOLEMAN

0342 **JULIA ANDRUS**

0343 JENNIFER ACKERMAN, DILLON DESIGNS

0344 HI ANNIE DESIGNS

0345 JULIA ANDRUS

0346 ANN WIDNER

0347 LINDA O'BRIEN

0348 VANDA NORONHA, PARAPHERNALIA.NU

0349 TIGERGIRL.ETSY.COM

0350 JANE McGREGOR
HAMILTON MORMINO

0351 BRUNA VASCONCELOS

0352 PHAEDRA A. TORRES,
LLUVIA DESIGNS

0353 CRISTINA MANHENTE

0354 TRACEY H. THOMASSON

0355 PHAEDRA A. TORRES,
LLUVIA DESIGNS

0356 PHAEDRA A. TORRES, LLUVIA DESIGNS

0357 **LAUREN E. OCHMAN, THE LOLA COLLECTION**
PHOTO BY PATRICIA WALSH

0358 TIGERGIRL.ETSY.COM

0359 LAUREN E. OCHMAN,
THE LOLA COLLECTION
PHOTO BY PATRICIA WALSH

0360 DEBORAH FRANKS
ARTWORKS.ETSY.COM

0361 JANET BASKERVILLE, JBASK ARTS
PHOTO BY MICHAEL J. JOYCE

0362 VICKIE ZUMPF

0363 ANDREIA CUNHA MARTINS

0364 JANET HICKEY

0365 JULIA ANDRUS

0366 PRETTY•FUN

0367 STEPHANIE LEE

0368 CAROL KEMP, CAROL K. ORIGINALS

0369 NANCY ANDERSON, SWEET BIRD STUDIO

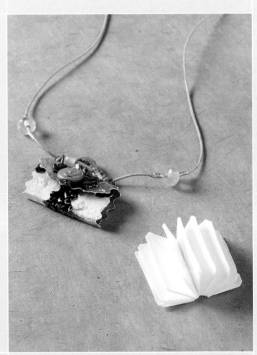

0370 CAROL KEMP, CAROL K. ORIGINALS

0371 CAROL KEMP, CAROL K. ORIGINALS

0372 CAROL KEMP, CAROL K. ORIGINALS

0373 AMY HELM

0374 LORI LARSON

0375 JENNIFER ACKERMAN, DILLON DESIGNS

0376 ELENA MARY SIFF, ELENAMARY.ETSY.COM

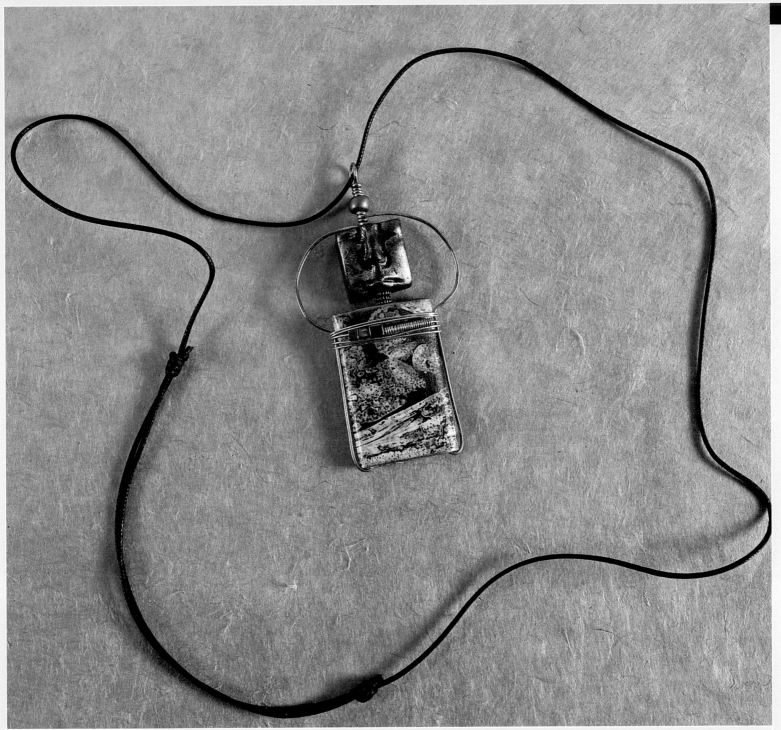

0377 PAM SANDERS

0378 MARCIA ACKER-MISSALL

0379 NANCY ANDERSON,
SWEET BIRD STUDIO

0380 JANET BASKERVILLE, JBASK ARTS
PHOTO BY MICHAEL J. JOYCE

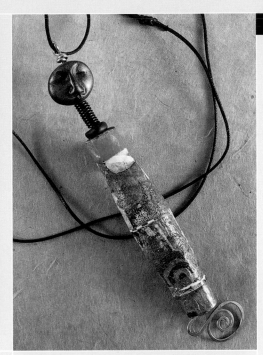

0381 PAM SANDERS

0382 IVORY EILEEN,
PAPER ORGANICS JEWELRY

0383 PRETTY•FUN

0384 JANET BASKERVILLE, JBASK ARTS
PHOTO BY MICHAEL J. JOYCE

0385 PHAEDRA A. TORRES,
LLUVIA DESIGNS

0386 PHAEDRA A. TORRES,
LLUVIA DESIGNS

0387 PHAEDRA A. TORRES,
LLUVIA DESIGNS

0388 IVORY EILEEN,
PAPER ORGANICS JEWELRY

0389 LORI LARSON

0390 MODERNJEWELRYART.COM

0391 CAROL KEMP, CAROL K. ORIGINALS

0392 CAROL KEMP, CAROL K. ORIGINALS

0393 IVORY EILEEN,
PAPER ORGANICS JEWELRY

0394 WE DREAM IN COLOUR

0395   ELLENE McCLAY

0396 NANCY ANDERSON, SWEET BIRD STUDIO

0397 MOOD SWING

0398 PHAEDRA A. TORRES, LLUVIA DESIGNS

0399 TERI DEGINSTIEN, MIDNIGHTBLUART

0400 NANCY ANDERSON, SWEET BIRD STUDIO

0401 NANCY ANDERSON, SWEET BIRD STUDIO

0402   KIONA WILSON,
        LUCKY ACCESSORIES

0403   JANE McGREGOR
        HAMILTON MORMINO

0404   STEPHANIE LEE

0405   LORI LARSON

0406   TARA MANNING FINLAY

0407   HELOISE

0408 MICHELA VERANI

0410 TERI DEGINSTIEN, MIDNIGHTBLUART

0411 MIA GOFAR JEWELRY

0412 OPIE O'BRIEN

0413 WE DREAM IN COLOUR

0414 LAUREN E. OCHMAN, THE LOLA COLLECTION
PHOTO BY PATRICIA WALSH

0415 TERI DEGINSTIEN, MIDNIGHTBLUART

0416 LAUREN E. OCHMAN, THE LOLA COLLECTION
PHOTO BY PATRICIA WALSH

0417 DEBORAH BOGDAN, FLAWED FLOCK
PHOTO BY MICHAEL BOGDAN

0418 THE WEEKEND STORE BY ADJOWAH BRODY

0419 JANET BASKERVILLE, JBASK ARTS
PHOTO BY MICHAEL J. JOYCE

0420 WE DREAM IN COLOUR

0421 CAROL KEMP, CAROL K. ORIGINALS

0422 CAROL LISTENBERGER

0423 TARA MANNING FINLAY

0424 CAROL LISTENBERGER

0425 CYNDI LAVIN

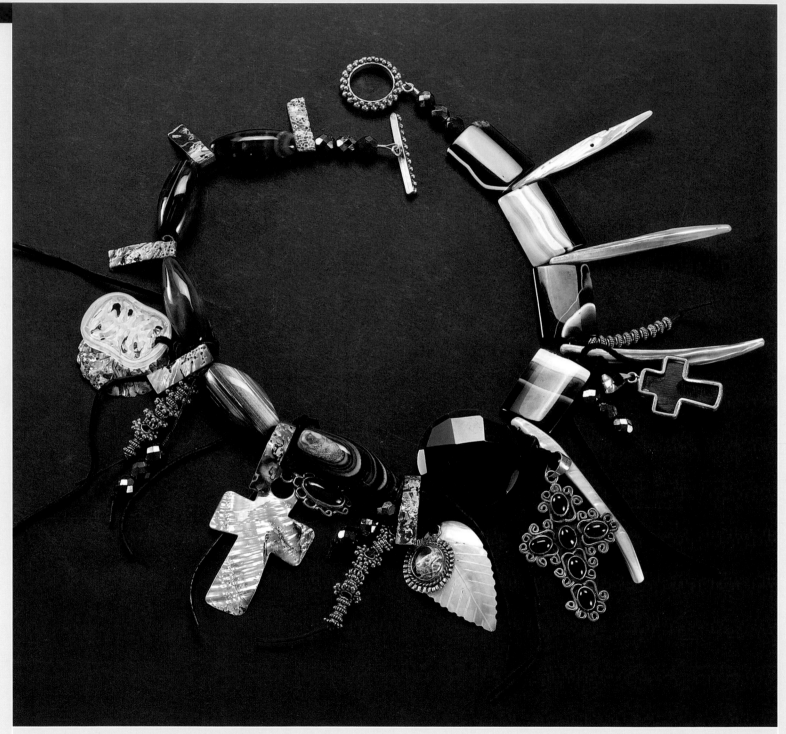

0426 PHAEDRA A. TORRES, LLUVIA DESIGNS

0427 ROSEBONBON

0428 AMY HELM

0429 SHARI BONNIN

0430 WE DREAM IN COLOUR

0431 JANET BASKERVILLE, JBASK ARTS
PHOTO BY MICHAEL J. JOYCE

0432 ROSEBONBON

0433 IVORY EILEEN, PAPER ORGANICS JEWELRY

0434 DONNA GARSIDE CASON

0435 PHAEDRA A. TORRES, LLUVIA DESIGNS

0436 ELIZABETH GLASS GELTMAN, RACHEL GELTMAN
+ NOAH MACMILLAN

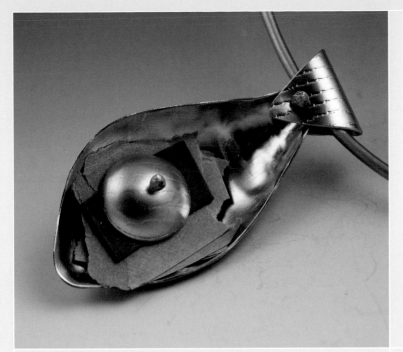

0437 ELIZABETH GLASS GELTMAN + RACHEL GELTMAN

0438 LORI LARSON

0439 TARA MANNING FINLAY

0440 MICHELA VERANI

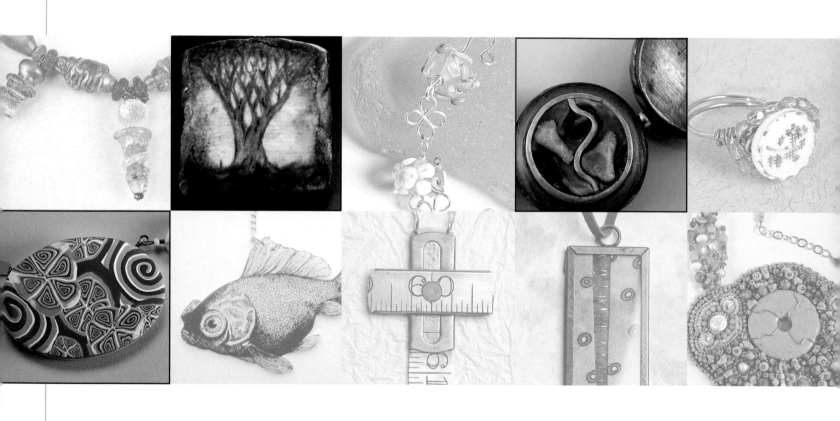

polymer +
precious metal clay

chapter 3

0441 SHANNON LeVART

0442 MICHELE GARRETT-GESING
PHOTO BY CHRIS LAMBRIGHT

0443 LYNNE ANN SCHWARZENBERG

0444 SHANNON LeVART

0445 LORI SCOUTON

0446 LORI SCOUTON

0447 LORI SCOUTON

0448 MARCIA PALMER

0449 BETSY BAKER, STONEHOUSE STUDIO

0450 MAUREEN THOMAS DESIGNS

0451 LYNNE ANN SCHWARZENBERG

0452 MARCIA PALMER

0453 MARCIA PALMER

0454 MADE IN LOWELL

0455 DAWN BARKER,
HARDFLOWER STUDIOS

0456 DARLEEN BELLAN,
KISSMYSTAMP DESIGNS

0457 MARCIA PALMER

0458 BETSY BAKER,
STONEHOUSE STUDIO

0459 RACHEL PRYDEN

0460 SHANNON LeVART

0461 TERI DEGINSTIEN, MIDNIGHTBLUART

0462 TAMARA SHEA, BLOCK PARTY PRESS

0463 LITTLE SHEEP, LITTLESHEEP.ETSY.COM

0464 CANDY STILL

0465 STUDIO BIJOU

0466 TAMARA SHEA, BLOCK PARTY PRESS

0467 MARIA DIANA

0468 TAMARA SHEA, BLOCK PARTY PRESS

0469 MARCIA PALMER

0470 DAWN BARKER, HARDFLOWER STUDIOS

0471 MARIA DIANA

0472 MAUREEN THOMAS DESIGNS

0473 MICHELE GARRETT-GESING
PHOTO BY CHRIS LAMBRIGHT

0474 TAMARA SHEA, BLOCK PARTY PRESS

0475 LYNNE ANN SCHWARZENBERG

0476 ANN ANTANAVAGE, MISS DANCEY PANTS

0477 TAMARA SHEA, BLOCK PARTY PRESS

0478 ADORN, SANDY SNEAD

0479 CANDY STILL

0480 BETSY BAKER, STONEHOUSE STUDIO

0481 MADE IN LOWELL

0482 SHANNON LeVART

0483 ADORN, SANDY SNEAD

0484 CANDY STILL

0485 MADE IN LOWELL

0486 **LAUREN E. OCHMAN, THE LOLA COLLECTION**
PHOTO BY PATRICIA WALSH

0487 **LAUREN E. OCHMAN, THE LOLA COLLECTION**
PHOTO BY PATRICIA WALSH

0488 **LAUREN E. OCHMAN, THE LOLA COLLECTION**
PHOTO BY PATRICIA WALSH

0489 **LAUREN E. OCHMAN, THE LOLA COLLECTION**
PHOTO BY PATRICIA WALSH

0490 LAUREN E. OCHMAN, THE LOLA COLLECTION
PHOTO BY PATRICIA WALSH

0491 LAUREN E. OCHMAN, THE LOLA COLLECTION
PHOTO BY PATRICIA WALSH

0492 LAUREN E. OCHMAN, THE LOLA COLLECTION
PHOTO BY PATRICIA WALSH

0493 LAUREN E. OCHMAN, THE LOLA COLLECTION
PHOTO BY PATRICIA WALSH

0494 PHAEDRA A. TORRES, LLUVIA DESIGNS

0495 BETSY BAKER,
STONEHOUSE STUDIO

0496 BETSY BAKER,
STONEHOUSE STUDIO

0497 DAWN BARKER,
HARDFLOWER STUDIOS

0498 MARCIA PALMER

0499 JANA ROBERTS BENZON

0500 BETSY BAKER,
STONEHOUSE STUDIO

0501 DAWN BARKER, HARDFLOWER STUDIOS

0502 DAWN BARKER, HARDFLOWER STUDIOS

0503 DAWN BARKER, HARDFLOWER STUDIOS

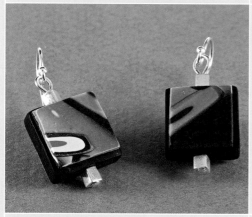

0504 MAUREEN THOMAS DESIGNS

0505 DAWN BARKER, HARDFLOWER STUDIOS

0506 HOLLY PIPER-SMITH, POLLYHYPER.ETSY.COM

0507 PAM SANDERS

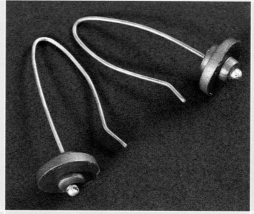

0508 DAWN BARKER, HARDFLOWER STUDIOS

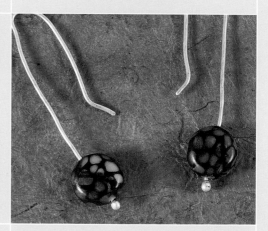

0509 DAWN BARKER, HARDFLOWER STUDIOS

0510 GERALDINE NEWFRY

LYNNE ANN SCHWARZENBERG

0512 MARCIA PALMER

0513 MARCIA PALMER

0514 MARCIA PALMER

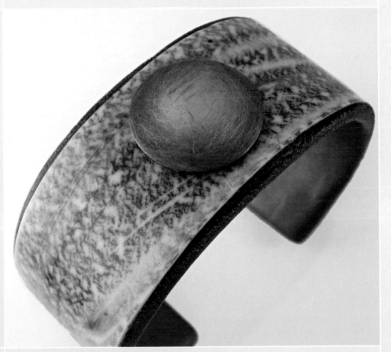

0515 BETSY BAKER, STONEHOUSE STUDIO

0516 MARCIA PALMER

0517 HOLLY PIPER-SMITH,
POLLYHYPER.ETSY.COM

0518 MICHELA VERANI

0519 BEAD JEWELRY BY SHOPGIRL

0520 TAMARA SHEA,
BLOCK PARTY PRESS

0521 DAWN BARKER,
HARDFLOWER STUDIOS

0523 ZUDA GAY PEASE, ZUDAGAY.ETSY.COM

0524 REBECCA TENACE,
CLAYARTIST.NET

0525 ANN ANTANAVAGE,
MISS DANCEY PANTS

0526 TAMARA SHEA,
BLOCK PARTY PRESS

0527 TAMARA SHEA,
BLOCK PARTY PRESS

0528 MICHELE GARRETT-GESING
PHOTO BY CHRIS LAMBRIGHT

0529 MADE IN LOWELL

0530 REBECCA TENACE,
CLAYARTIST.NET

0531 TAMARA SHEA, BLOCK PARTY PRESS

0532 PAM SANDERS

0533 TAMARA SHEA,
BLOCK PARTY PRESS

0534 BEAD JEWELRY BY SHOPGIRL

0535 TAMARA SHEA,
BLOCK PARTY PRESS

0536 CANDY STILL

0537 MICHELE GARRETT-GESING
PHOTO BY CHRIS LAMBRIGHT

0538 DAWN BARKER,
HARDFLOWER STUDIOS

0539 CAROL KEMP, CAROL K. ORIGINALS

0540 LYNNE ANN SCHWARZENBERG

0541 MICHELE GARRETT-GESING
PHOTO BY CHRIS LAMBRIGHT

0542 LYNNE ANN SCHWARZENBERG

0543 CANDY STILL

0544 STUDIO BIJOU

0545 DAWN BARKER,
HARDFLOWER STUDIOS

0546 ZUDA GAY PEASE
ZUDAGAY.ETSY.COM

0547 ANN ANTANAVAGE,
MISS DANCEY PANTS

0548 MAUREEN THOMAS DESIGNS

0549 MADE IN LOWELL

0550 ZUDA GAY PEASE,
ZUDAGAY.ETSY.COM

0551 SHANNON LeVART

0552 CANDY STILL

0553 LESYA BINKIN

0554 MADE IN LOWELL

0555 REBECCA TENACE,
CLAYARTIST.NET

0556 MADE IN LOWELL

0557 INEDIBLE JEWELRY

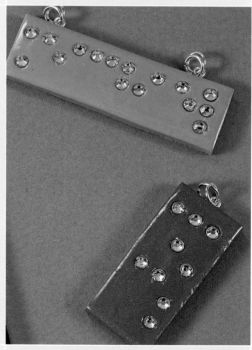

0558 JULIE DUTT,
JULIE*ANN HANDMADE GOODS

0559 ANN ANTANAVAGE, MISS DANCEY PANTS

0560 MAUREEN THOMAS DESIGNS

0561 BETSY BAKER, STONEHOUSE STUDIO

0562 ADORN, SANDY SNEAD

0563 JANA ROBERTS BENZON

0564 STUDIO BIJOU

0565 STUDIO BIJOU

0566 MICHELE GARRETT-GESING
PHOTO BY CHRIS LAMBRIGHT

0567 BETSY BAKER, STONEHOUSE STUDIO

0568   MARCIA PALMER

0569 HOLLY PIPER-SMITH, POLLYHYPER.ETSY.COM

0570 DAWN BARKER, HARDFLOWER STUDIOS

0571 BETSY BAKER, STONEHOUSE STUDIO

0572 BETSY BAKER, STONEHOUSE STUDIO

0573 JANA ROBERTS BENZON

0574 JANA ROBERTS BENZON

0575 JANA ROBERTS BENZON

0576 JANA ROBERTS BENZON

0577 JANA ROBERTS BENZON

0578 LESYA BINKIN

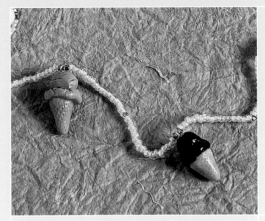

0579 INEDIBLE JEWELRY

0580 MADE IN LOWELL

0581 HOLLY PIPER-SMITH,
POLLYHYPER.ETSY.COM

0582 DAWN BARKER,
HARDFLOWER STUDIOS

0583 INEDIBLE JEWELRY

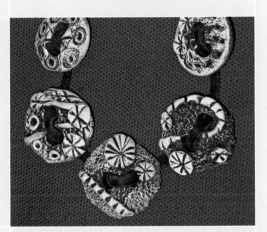

0584 TANYA BESEDINA

0585 HOLLY PIPER-SMITH
POLLYHYPER.ETSY.COM

0586 JULIE DUTT,
JULIE*ANN HANDMADE GOODS

0587 INEDIBLE JEWELRY

0588 JULIE DUTT,
JULIE*ANN HANDMADE GOODS

0589 JACKIE WAIK-ATIYA

0590 CAROL LISTENBERGER

0591 ANN ANTANAVAGE, MISS DANCEY
PANTS

0592 SANDRA TATSUKO KADOWAKI

0593 RONDA KIVETT

0594 INEDIBLE JEWELRY

0595 JULIE DUTT,
JULIE*ANN HANDMADE GOODS

0596 JACKIE WAIK-ATIYA

0597 ZUDA GAY PEASE, ZUDAGAY.ETSY.COM

0598 TONI M. RANSFIELD

0599   GERALDINE NEWFRY

0600   SANDRA TATSUKO KADOWAKI

0601   MICHELA VERANI

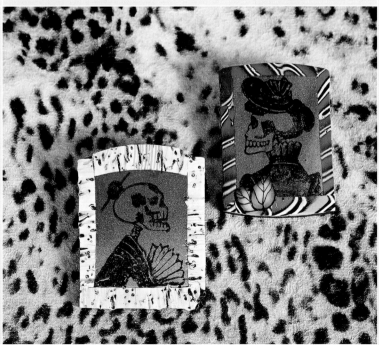

0602   DARLEEN BELLAN, KISSMYSTAMP DESIGNS

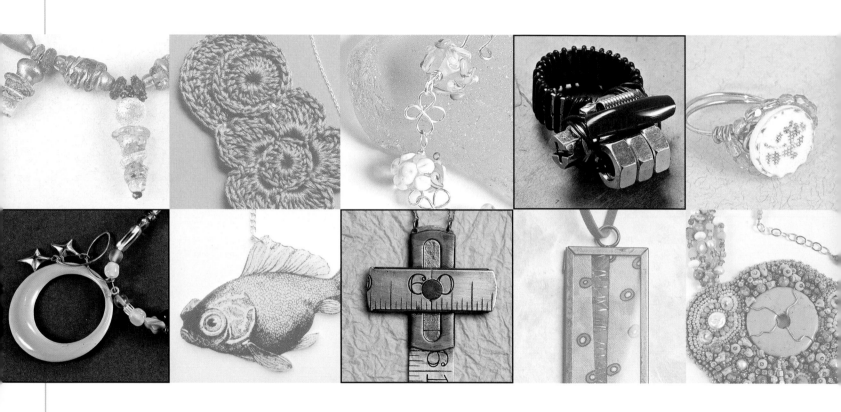

vintage + repurposed

chapter 4

0603-0749

0603 PAPER FLOWER GIRL

0604 KARIBETH.COM

0605 JANET BASKERVILLE, JBASK ARTS
PHOTO BY MICHAEL J. JOYCE

0606 JANET BASKERVILLE, JBASK ARTS
PHOTO BY MICHAEL J. JOYCE

0607 PEQUITOBUN

0608 SANDRA SALAMONY

0609 PAPER FLOWER GIRL

0610 ARMOUR SANS ANGUISH

0611 MOOD SWING

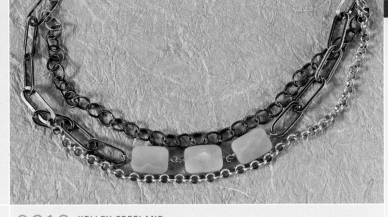

0612 KELLEY FREELAND

0613 MOOD SWING

0614 KIONA WILSON, LUCKY ACCESSORIES

0615 ARMOUR SANS ANGUISH

0616 KELLEY FREELAND

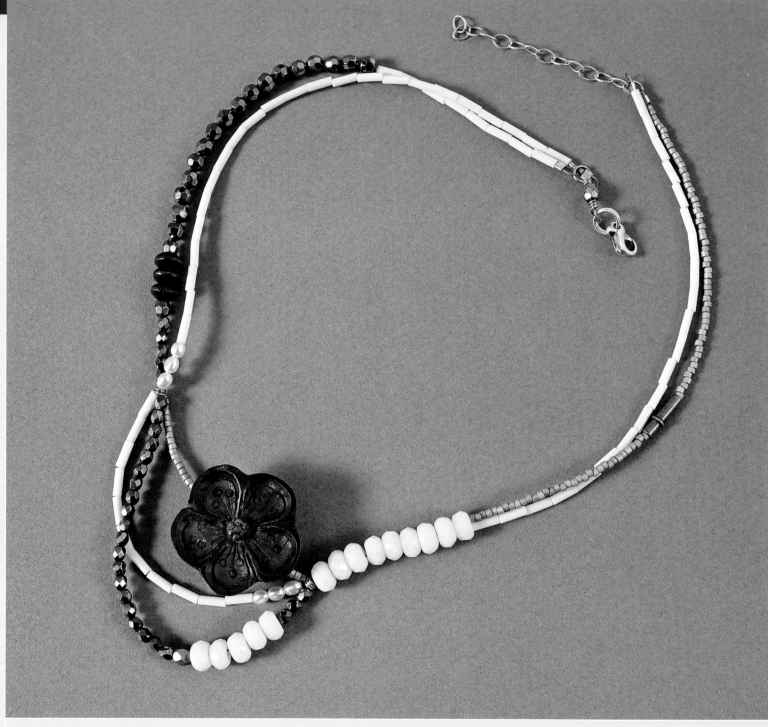

0617 KELLEY FREELAND

0618 DENISE WITMER

0619 MIGGIPYN, DIANE WADE

0620 KELLEY FREELAND

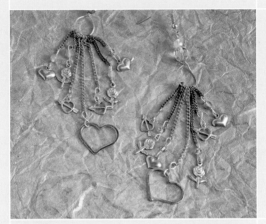

0621 MIGGIPYN, DIANE WADE

0622 MIGGIPYN, DIANE WADE

0623 CYNDI LAVIN

0624 PHAEDRA A. TORRES,
LLUVIA DESIGNS

0625 MICHELA VERANI

0626 TIGERGIRL.ETSY.COM

0627 KARIBETH.COM

0628 SANDRA SALAMONY

0629 PEQUITOBUN

0630 JULIA ANDRUS

0632 PEQUITOBUN

0633 PEQUITOBUN

0634 PEQUITOBUN

0635 PEQUITOBUN

0636 PEQUITOBUN

0637 PEQUITOBUN

0638 PEQUITOBUN

0640 JENNIFER PERKINS

0641 THERESA MINK DESIGNS

0642 KARIBETH.COM

0643 JODI BLOOM

0644 MOOD SWING

0645 TIGERGIRL.ETSY.COM

0646 WE DREAM IN COLOUR

0647 MOOD SWING

0648 KARIBETH.COM

0649 ARMOUR SANS ANGUISH

0650 MOOD SWING

0651 PEQUITOBUN

0652 PEQUITOBUN

0653 PEQUITOBUN

0654 ERIN SARGEANT, LIKE A FOX

0655 ANDREA DREYER

0656 ANDREA DREYER

0657 ANDREA DREYER

0658 ANDREA DREYER

0659 ANDREA DREYER

0660 ANDREA DREYER

0661 VICTORIA BUTTON

0662 NIKI MALEK, STELLA + LUX

0663 PEQUITOBUN

0664 KARIBETH.COM

0665 MIGGIPYN, DIANE WADE

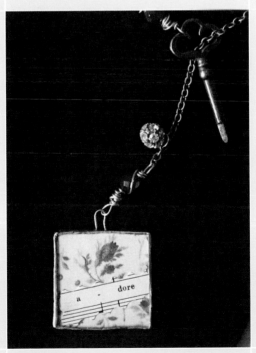

0666 JANET BASKERVILLE, JBASK ARTS
PHOTO BY MICHAEL J. JOYCE

0667 TIGERGIRL.ETSY.COM

0668　MIGGIPYN, DIANE WADE

0669　PAPER FLOWER GIRL

0670　KARIBETH.COM

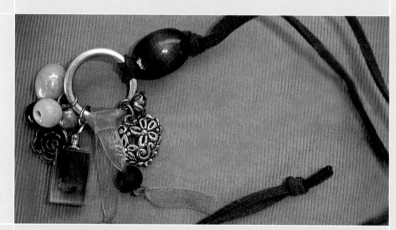

0671　ROSEBONBON

0672　ELENA MARIE SIFF, ELENAMARIE.ETSY.COM

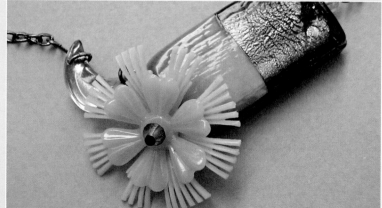

0673　TIGERGIRL.ETSY.COM

0674 CYNDI LAVIN

0675 ERIN SARGEANT, LIKE A FOX

0676 KARIBETH.COM

0677 ROSEBONBON

0678 TIGERGIRL.ETSY.COM

0679 MOOD SWING

0680 TARA FEENEY, LEVITICUSJEWELRY.COM

0681 TARA FEENEY, LEVITICUSJEWELRY.COM

0682 MOOD SWING

0683 RELISHDRESS

0684 NICOLE NOELLE

0685 WE DREAM IN COLOUR

0686 BEATRIZ SOUZA
PHOTO BY MARCELO CÉLIO

0687 MADE IN LOWELL

0688 WE DREAM IN COLOUR

0689 MADE IN LOWELL

0690 TARA MANNING FINLAY

0691　IVORY EILEEN, PAPER ORGANICS JEWELRY

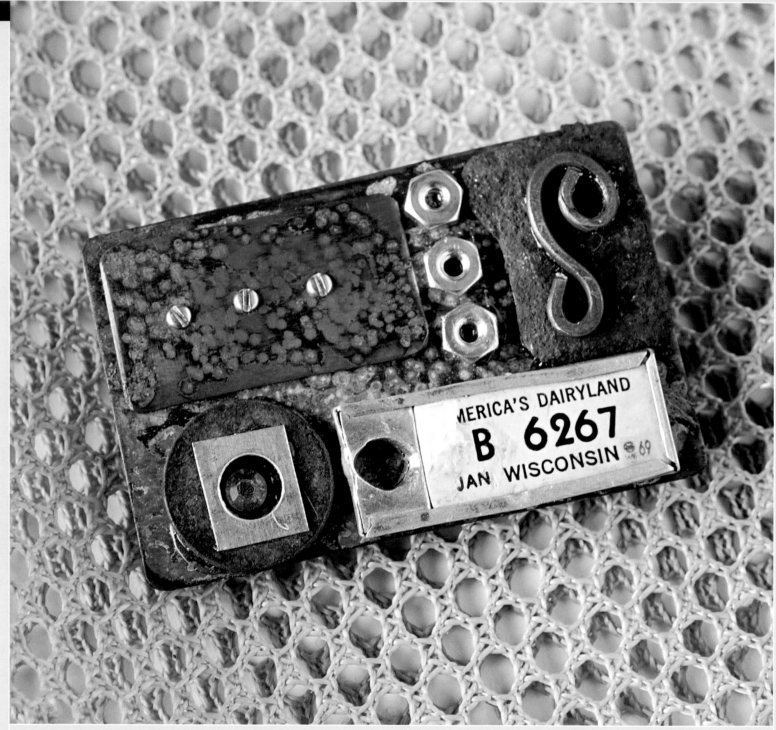

0692 LORI LARSON

0693 LAURA SANTONE, SHESHA

0694 ANDREIA CUNHA MARTINS

0695 TERI DEGINSTIEN, MIDNIGHTBLUART

0696 ANDREIA CUNHA MARTINS

0697 LAURA SANTONE, SHESHA

0698 RELISHDRESS

0699 PHAEDRA A. TORRES, LLUVIA DESIGNS

0700 SARAH GORDEN, SOJOURN CURIOSITIES

0701 SHERRI FORRESTER

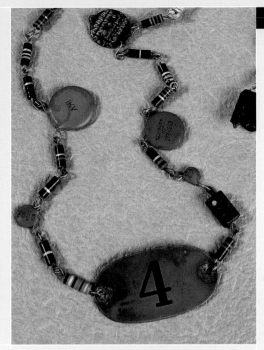

0702 SHERRI FORRESTER

0703 ELENA MARIE SIFF, ELENAMARIE.ETSY.COM

0704 DANA LYNN DRISCOLL

0705 LORI LARSON

0706 LAURA SANTONE, SHESHA

0707 JANET HICKEY

0708 DANA LYNN DRISCOLL

0709 HI ANNIE DESIGNS

0710 LAURA SANTONE, SHESHA

0711 JANET HICKEY

0712   DEBORAH FRANKS, ARTWORKS.ETSY.COM

0713 MITZI WEILAND

0714 SANDRA SALAMONY

0715 PHAEDRA A. TORRES,
LLUVIA DESIGNS

0716 MIA GOFAR JEWELRY

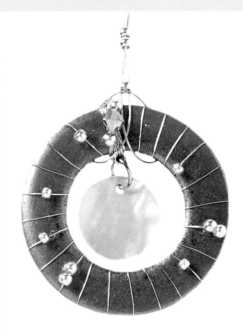

0717 ELENA MARIE SIFF,
ELENAMARIE.ETSY.COM

0718 ELIZABETH DICKINSON

0719 PHAEDRA A. TORRES,
LLUVIA DESIGNS

0720 SHERRI FORRESTER

0721 THE WEEKEND STORE
BY ADJOWAH BRODY

0722 JANET BASKERVILLE, JBASK ARTS
PHOTO BY MICHAEL J. JOYCE

0723 JANET BASKERVILLE, JBASK ARTS
PHOTO BY MICHAEL J. JOYCE

0724 THE WEEKEND STORE
BY ADJOWAH BRODY

0725 SHERRI FORRESTER

0726 HALLE GUSTAFSON

0727 TOMATE D'EPINGLES, GUYLAINE MARTINEAU, TOMATEDEPINGLES.ETSY.COM

0728 JANET BASKERVILLE, JBASK ARTS
PHOTO BY MICHAEL J. JOYCE

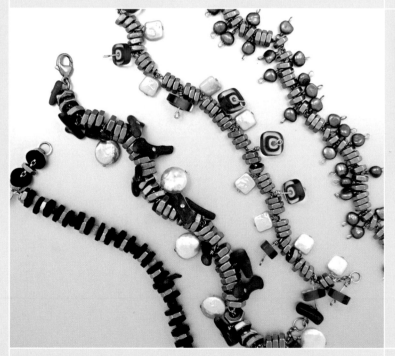

0729 NICOLE NOELLE

0730 SHERRI FORRESTER

0731 THE WEEKEND STORE
BY ADJOWAH BRODY

0732 JENNY LOUGHMILLER

0733 REUBEN MILLER

0734 ELLENE McCLAY

0735 ENRICA PRAZZOLI

0736 LAURA SANTONE, SHESHA

0737 LAURA SANTONE, SHESHA

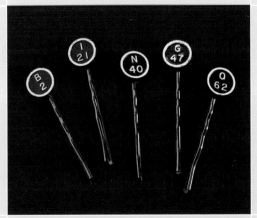

0738 THE WEEKEND STORE
BY ADJOWAH BRODY

0739 NICOLE NOELLE

0740 JANET BASKERVILLE, JBASK ARTS
PHOTO BY MICHAEL J. JOYCE

0741 THE WEEKEND STORE BY ADJOWAH BRODY

0742 THE WEEKEND STORE BY ADJOWAH BRODY

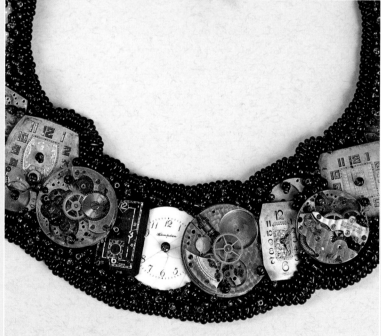

0743 CYNDI LAVIN

0744 ANDREIA CUNHA MARTINS

0745 MEREAM PACAYRA

0746 SHERRI FORRESTER

0747 THE WEEKEND STORE
BY ADJOWAH BRODY

0748 ENRICA PRAZZOLI

0749 HELOISE

0750 CAROL LISTENBERGER

0751 TARA TURNER

0752 MIA GOFAR JEWELRY

0753 JENNI PAGANO

0754 ROSEBONBON

0755 PAPER FLOWER GIRL

0756 SHARI BONNIN

0757 PAPER FLOWER GIRL

0758 CRISTINA MANHENTE

0759 MADE IN LOWELL

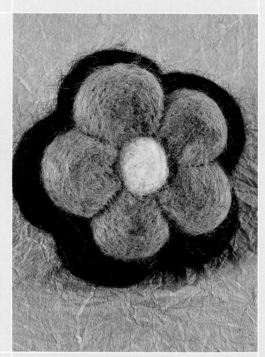

0760 KELLEY FREELAND

0761   PAPER FLOWER GIRL

0762   MIGGIPYN, DIANE WADE

0763 SHARI BONNIN

0764 JANET BASKERVILLE, JBASK ARTS
PHOTO BY MICHAEL J. JOYCE

0765 THE WHITE SHEEP

0766 STEPHANIE RIGER JEWELRY,
STEPHANIERIGER.COM

0767 MADE IN LOWELL

0768 MIA GOFAR JEWELRY

0769 KNITTING GURU, VEENA BURRY

0770 RELISHDRESS

0771 LINDSAY STREEM

0772 LINDSAY STREEM

0773 PAPER FLOWER GIRL

0774 CURSIVE DESIGN

0775 WANDRWEDDING BY WENDY

0776 WANDRWEDDING BY WENDY

0778 LINDSAY STREEM

0779 HELOISE

0780 LORI LARSON

0781 HELOISE

0782 DEBORAH FRANKS,
ARTWORKS.ETSY.COM

0783 ROSEBONBON

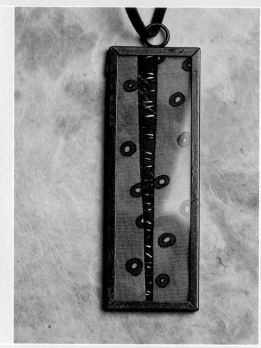

0784 KNITTING GURU, VEENA BURRY

0785 THE WHITE SHEEP

0786 JENNY LOUGHMILLER

0787 PAPER FLOWER GIRL

0788 ADORN, SANDY SNEAD

0789 PAPER FLOWER GIRL

0790   JILL BLISS, BLISSEN.COM

0791   ADORN, SANDY SNEAD

0792 PAPER FLOWER GIRL

0793 JENNI PAGANO

0794 JENNI PAGANO

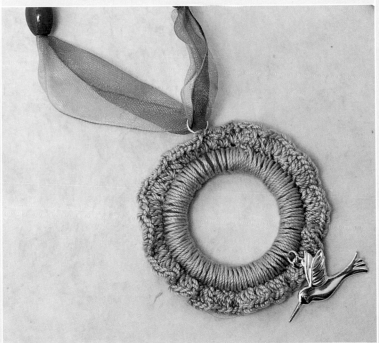

0795 LINDSAY STREEM

0796 PAPER FLOWER GIRL

0797 RELISHDRESS

0798 KNITTING GURU, VEENA BURRY

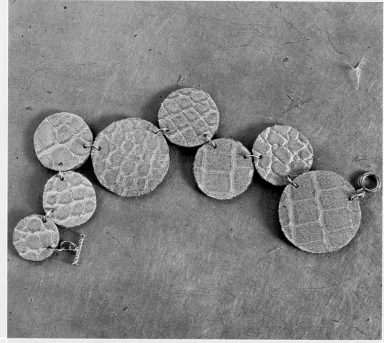

0799 KELLIOPE

0800 AI-LING CHANG

0801 KNITTING GURU, VEENA BURRY

0802 RELISHDRESS

0803 LINDSAY STREEM

0804 MADE IN LOWELL

0805 DIANA SAMPER

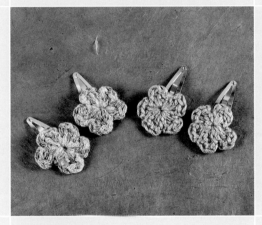

0806 LINDSAY STREEM

0807 RELISHDRESS

0808 DIANA SAMPER

0809 JACKIE WAIK-ATIYA

0810 PAPER FLOWER GIRL

0811   LISA LAMPE

0812   MANDALA JEWELS,
         MANDALAJEWELS.ETSY.COM

0813   PHAEDRA A. TORRES, LLUVIA DESIGNS

0814   BELLE POUR LA VIE,
         BELLEPOURLAVIE.COM

0815   RUBY CHAN

0816   ARMOUR SANS ANGUISH

CAROL LISTENBERGER

0818 RELISHDRESS

0819 ROSEBONBON

0820 AMY HELM

0821 ZONA SHERMAN.
TWIRL GIRL FIBERS

0822 KELLIOPE

0823 CAROL LISTENBERGER

0824 RELISHDRESS

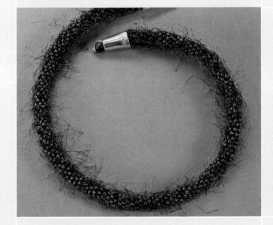

0825 CAROL A. BABINEAU,
ART CLAY STUDIO

0826 BELLE POUR LA VIE,
BELLEPOURLAVIE.COM

0827 CURSIVE DESIGN

0828 ANA PEREIRA

0829 PAPER FLOWER GIRL

0830 CRISTINA MANHENTE

0831 DEBORAH FRANKS
ARTWORKS.ETSY.COM

0832 CURSIVE DESIGN

0833 PEGGY PRIELOZNY

0834 AMY HELM

0835 ARMOUR SANS ANGUISH

0836 JILL BLISS, BLISSEN.COM

0837 HI ANNIE DESIGNS

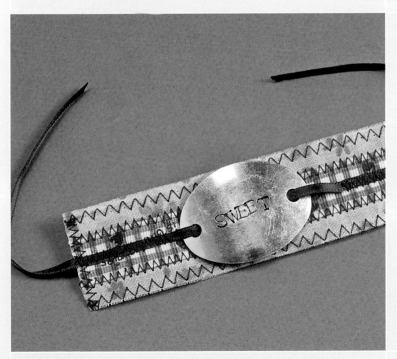

0838 HI ANNIE DESIGNS

0839 MIGGIPYN, DIANE WADE

0840 DEBRA POTH

0841 DEBRA POTH

0842 KNITTING GURU, VEENA BURRY

0843 DEBRA POTH

0844 CAROL LISTENBERGER

0845 LINDSAY STREEM

0846 CRISTINA MANHENTE

0847 CAROL LISTENBERGER

0848 DIANA SAMPER

0849 JENNI PAGANO

0850 JEANNE WERTMAN

0851 THE WHITE SHEEP

0852 CRISTINA MANHENTE

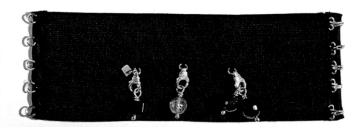

0853 OLGA NORONHA

0854 PAPER FLOWER GIRL

0855 LINDSAY STREEM

0856 KNITTING GURU, VEENA BURRY

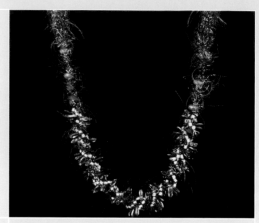

0857 KIARA M. McNULTY

0858 CURSIVE DESIGN

0859 LINDSAY STREEM

0860 RELISHDRESS

0861 MADE IN LOWELL

0862 RUBY CHAN

0863 DONNA GARSIDE CASON

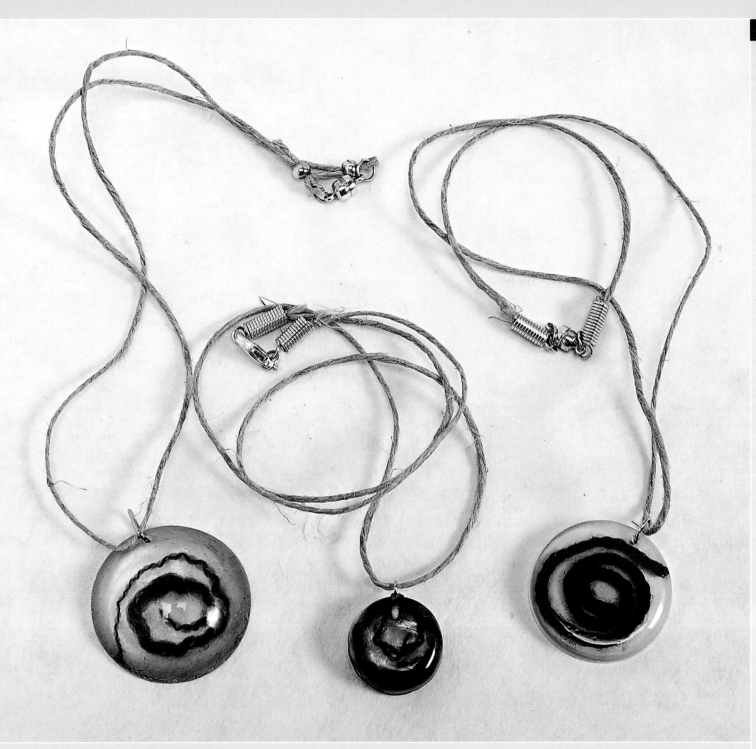

0864 ZONA SHERMAN, TWIRL GIRL FIBERS

wire + metal

chapter 6

0865 CYNTHIA ALVAREZ, CALUMEY DESIGNS

0866 KATHLEEN MALEY

0867 RELISHDRESS

0868 VICKY X. NGUYEN

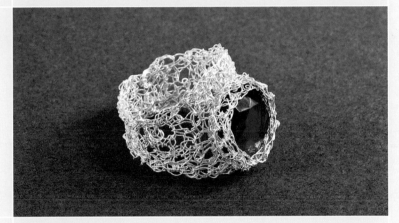

0869 GIOVANNA LEÓN

0870 JESSICA NEAVES

0871 SHARI BONNIN

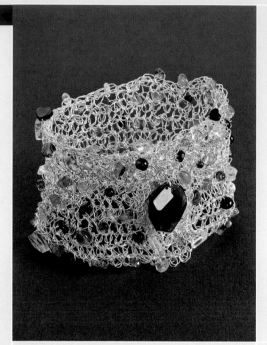

0872 LISA WEBER,
CRYSTAL WOMAN JEWELRY

0873 LISA NIVEN KELLY

0874 LISA LAMPE

0875 JQ JEWELRY DESIGNS

0876 LAURIE E. PANARIELLO

0877 ELIZABETH DICKINSON

0878 WOUND AROUND JEWELRY, K. YEARWOOD

0879   GRETCHEN S. SARRAZOLLA

0880   MONA SONG DESIGNS

0881   REUBEN MILLER

0882   RUBY FISCHER

0883   HI ANNIE DESIGNS

0884   OLGA NORONHA

0885   VICKY X. NGUYEN

0886   KAY LANCASHIRE, KAY'S ARTYCLES

0887   LISA WEBER,
CRYSTAL WOMAN JEWELRY

0888 LILI HALL, ARTEFACT

0889 LAURA BRACKEN

0890 PATRICIA SUMMERS,
OWLFEATHERSANDFLUFF.COM

0891 MIA GOFAR JEWELRY

0892 DAPHNE "D.D." HESS

0893 McFARLAND DESIGNS

0894 THERESA MINK DESIGNS

0895 YAEL MILLER DESIGN

0896 ROCCA DESIGNS,
CAROLINA ESTRADA

0897 AMY HARDY

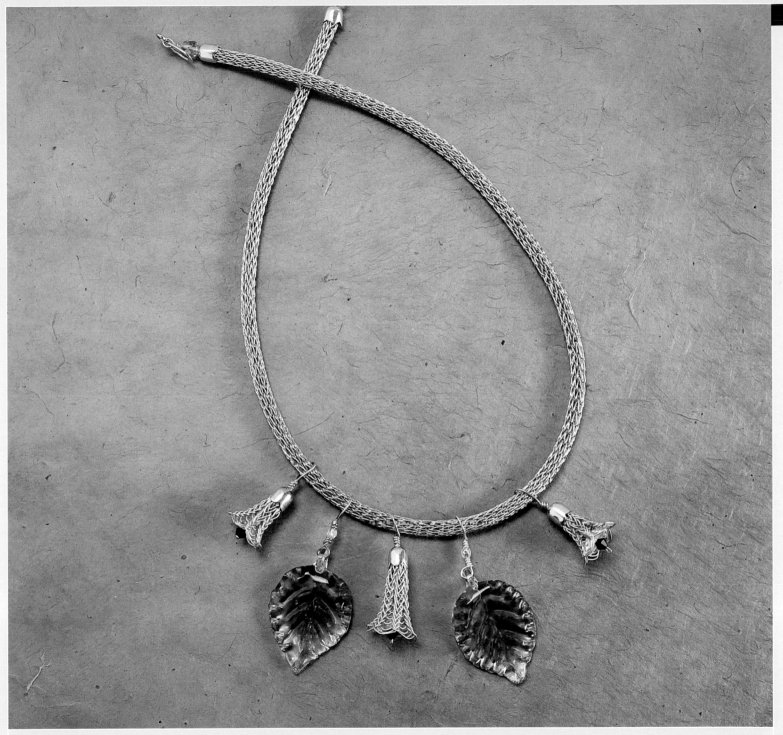

0898 KAY LANCASHIRE + BILL STRATHAM

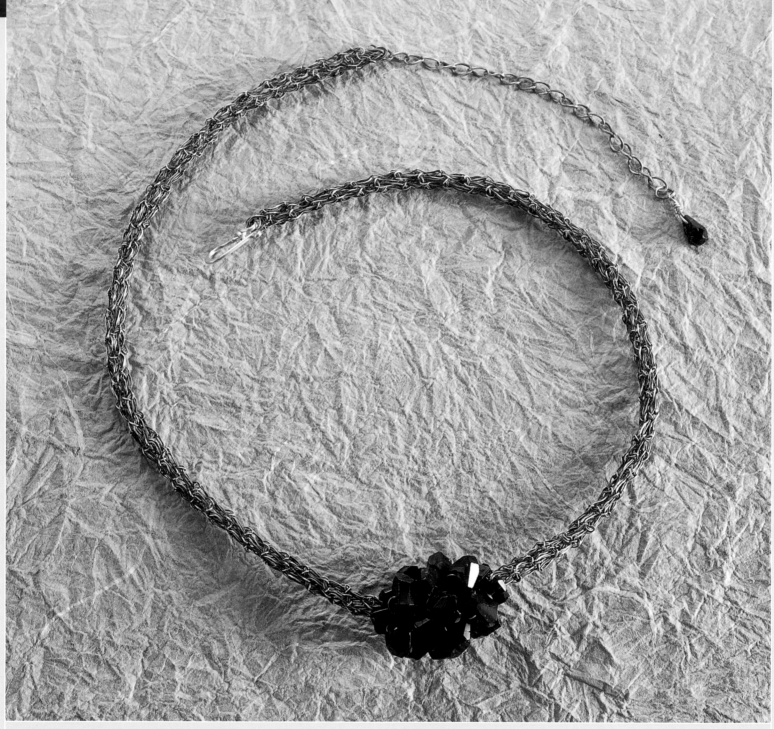

0899 PRECIOUS MESHES, EMILY CONROY

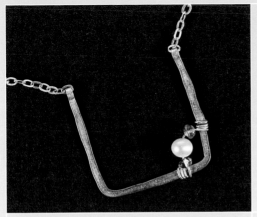

0900 ROCCA DESIGNS, CAROLINA ESTRADA

0901 MELISSA MUIR, KELSI'S CLOSET JEWELBOX

0902 WANDRDESIGN BY WENDY

0903 JANET HICKEY

0904 PRECIOUS MESHES, EMILY CONROY

0905 TAMMY POWLEY

0906 MONA SONG DESIGNS

0907 JENNY ZHOU

0908 MADE IN LOWELL

0909 ANA PEREIRA

0910 ANA PEREIRA

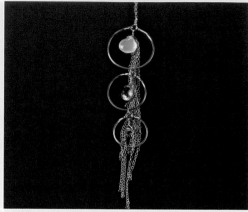

0911 MONA SONG DESIGNS

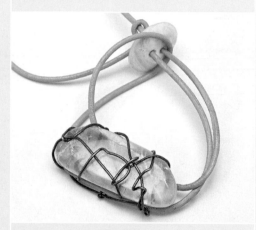

0912 BEATRIZ SOUZA
PHOTO BY MARCELO CÉLIO

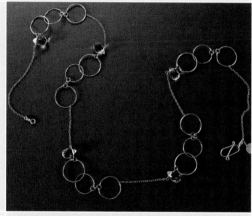

0913 MONA SONG DESIGNS

0914 RELISHDRESS

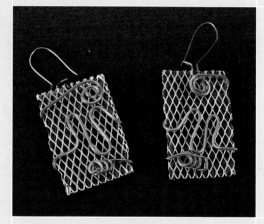

0915 BOBBY WERTMAN

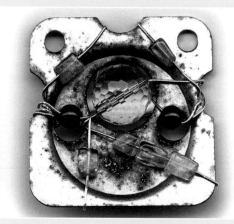

0916 YAEL MILLER DESIGN

0917 PAPER FLOWER GIRL

0918 ANDREIA CUNHA MARTINS

0919   OLGA NORONHA

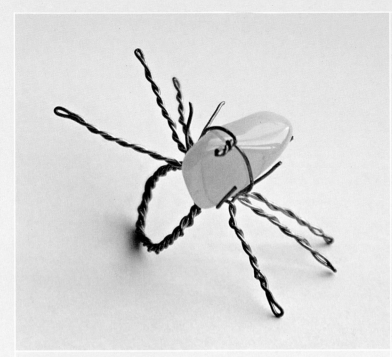

0920 OLGA NORONHA

0921 ANDREIA CUNHA MARTINS

0922 OLGA NORONHA

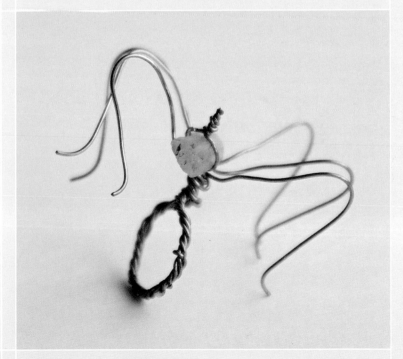

0923 OLGA NORONHA

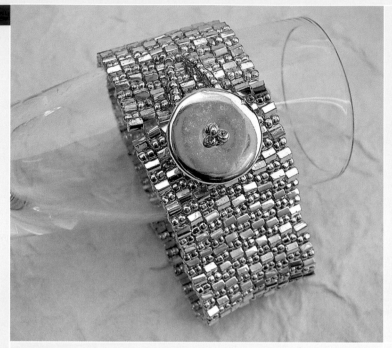

0924 BEAD JEWELRY BY SHOPGIRL

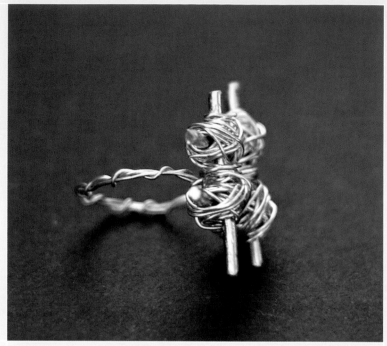

0925 ANDREIA CUNHA MARTINS

0926 GIOVANNA LEÓN

0927 ENI OKEN

0928 THE WEEKEND STORE BY ADJOWAH BRODY

0929 ANA PEREIRA

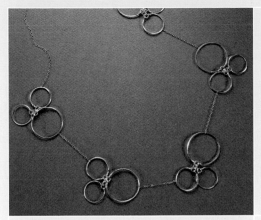

0930 MONA SONG DESIGNS

0931 PATRICIA SUMMERS,
OWLFEATHERSANDFLUFF.COM

0932 MELANI WILSON DESIGNS

0933 TARA MANNING FINLAY

0934 McFARLAND DESIGNS

0935 PRECIOUS MESHES,
EMILY CONROY

0936 SARAH GORDEN,
SOJOURN CURIOSITIES

0937 DAWN CECCACCI

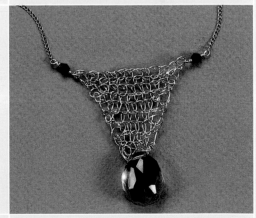

0938 PRECIOUS MESHES,
EMILY CONROY

0939 SHERRY J. INSLEY,
DANDELIONBLU JEWELRY

0940 RANDI SAMUELS

0941 SARAH GORDEN,
SOJOURN CURIOSITIES

0942 RUBY FISCHER

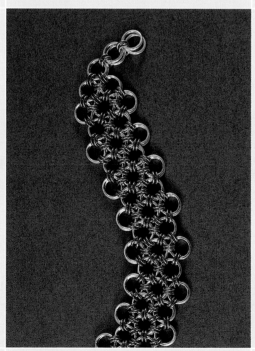

0943 RENEE THOMAS

0944 RANDI SAMUELS

RUBY FISCHER

0946 IRIS SANDKÜHLER

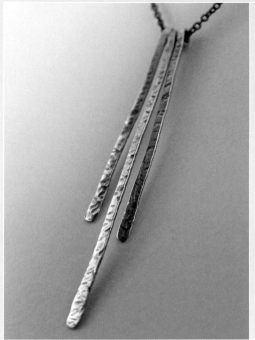

0947 SUSAN KUSLANSKY,
GODSAGA JEWELRY

0948 BELLE POUR LA VIE,
BELLEPOURLAVIE.COM

0949 CLARE L. STOKER-RING

0950 JEAN MARIE'S JEWELRY

0951 CLARE L. STOKER-RING

0952 JACKIE WAIK-ATIYA

0953 KIONA WILSON,
LUCKY ACCESSORIES

0954 LISA WEBER,
CRYSTAL WOMAN JEWELRY

0955 MONA SONG DESIGNS

0956 MODERNJEWELRYART.COM

0957 OLGA NORONHA

0958 AMY HELM

0959 NANCY ANDERSON, SWEET BIRD STUDIO

0960 NICOLE NOELLE

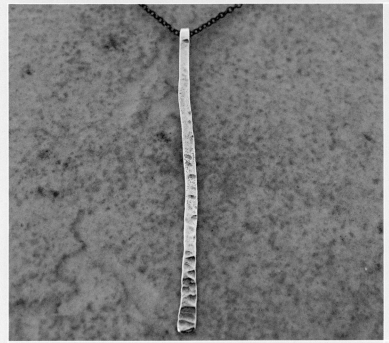

0961 SUSAN KUSLANSKY, GODSAGA JEWELRY

0962 TARA TURNER

0963 YAEL MILLER DESIGN

0964 TARA MANNING FINLAY

0965 ENI OKEN

0966 TRACEY H. THOMASSON

0967 TRACEY H. THOMASSON

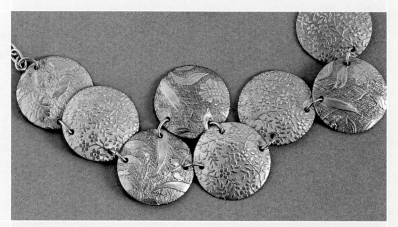

0968 KELLIOPE

0969 LISA WEBER, CRYSTAL WOMAN JEWELRY

0970 TAMMY POWLEY

0972 PAPER FLOWER GIRL

0973 WE DREAM IN COLOUR

0974 CATHERINE MARCHÉ

0975 AMY BOLING

0976 MODERNJEWELRYART.COM

0977 SHANNON LeVART

0978 CRISTINA MANHENTE

0979 PATRICIA SUMMERS,
OWLFEATHERSANDFLUFF.COM

0980 McFARLAND DESIGNS

0981 MONA SONG DESIGNS

0982 GARY L. HELWIG

0983 TRACY SUTHERLAND,
ORANGE STARFISH DESIGNS

0984 OLGA NORONHA

0985 MELISSA MUIR,
KELSI'S CLOSET JEWELBOX

0986 SARAH GORDEN,
SOJOURN CURIOSITIES

0987 LISA WEBER,
CRYSTAL WOMAN JEWELRY

0988 OLGA NORONHA

0989 AMY HARDY

0990 TAMMY POWLEY

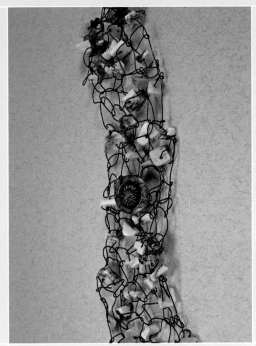

0991 SARAH GORDEN,
SOJOURN CURIOSITIES

0992 TARA MANNING FINLAY

0993 PATRICIA SUMMERS,
OWLFEATHERSANDFLUFF.COM

0994 JILL SHARP

0995 MONA SONG DESIGNS

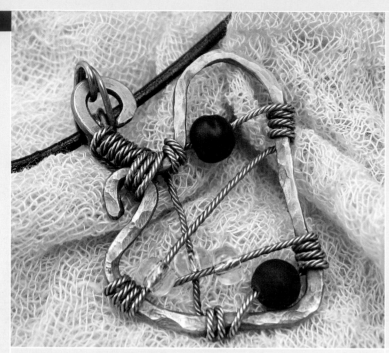

0996 DEBORAH FRANKS, ARTWORKS.ETSY.COM

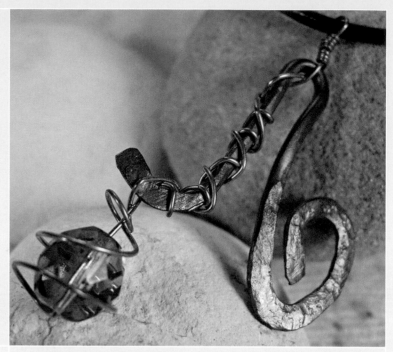

0997 DEBORAH FRANKS, ARTWORKS.ETSY.COM

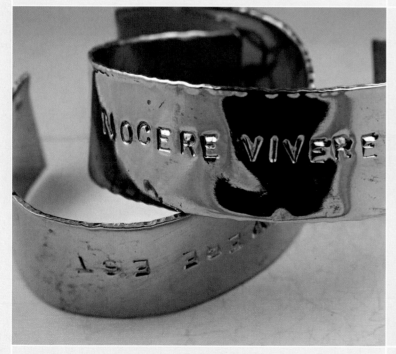

0998 ELIZABETH GLASS GELTMAN + RACHEL GELTMAN

0999 GIOVANNA LEÓN

1000 LILI HALL, ARTEFACT

APPENDIX:

jewelry-making techniques

It's amazing how many projects can be completed with a relatively small number of learned techniques. This appendix covers some of the fundamental jewelry-making techniques that will start creating your own handmade designs.

Basic jewelry findings can be purchased, but you can also craft your own from wire using simple tools. Here are a few to get you started:

EARRING FINDINGS

Basic beaded earrings are normally made up of an ear hook and a headpin. You will need round-nose pliers and wire cutters. For a basic beaded earring, use 21-gauge (0.71 mm), half-hard, round sterling wire. It's thin enough to go through a pierced hole in your ear and also fits through most beads, but it's also strong enough to handle the weight of the finished earring. Although it's a little thinner, 22-gauge (0.65 mm) also works well for most earring findings.

PROJECT 1: **BASIC EAR HOOKS**

This style of earring hook is often referred to as French wires or fishhooks. Whatever you call them, you only need a few hand tools and a few inches of wire to make a pair.

MATERIALS
3½" (8.75 cm) piece of wire
round-nose pliers
jeweler's file
wire cutters

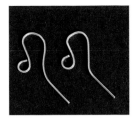

1. Begin by cutting your wire in half so that you have two pieces that are 1¾" (4.5 cm) each, and then use a jewelers' file to smooth the ends of each piece.

2. With round-nosed-pliers, create a small loop on one end of one piece of wire [A].

3. Repeat this for your other piece of wire, ensuring that the second loop is the same size as the first.

4. Next, hold both pieces of wire together so the loops are lined up right next to each other.

5. Grasp the straight part of your wires approximately ¼" (0.63 cm) past the loops with the thickest part of your round-nosed pliers, and use your fingers to bend both wires 180 degrees around the nose. You want to bend both wires at the same time to make your ear wires match [B].

6. The next step is a very small, subtle movement, but it will help make the hook a little more rounded. Using your round-nosed pliers, position the largest part of the nose inside the bent area, approximately ¼" (0.63 cm) from the curl. The pliers' nose should point up, and the wire curl should be positioned horizontally toward you. Gently squeeze the curl and flat part of ear hook toward each other about 5 degrees [C].

7. Hold both ear hooks side by side again. This time, use the middle area on the nose of your pliers, and measuring about ¼" (0.63 cm) away from the ends, slightly bend the ends of both wires (approximately 25 degrees) at the same time [D].

[A]

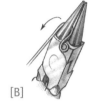

[B]

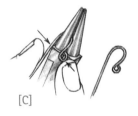

[C]

[D]

jeweler's tip:

If you're a little nervous about making your first pair of ear hooks, purchase a pair and use them as a guide or template while you work. As you make the ear hooks, refer occasionally to your purchased ear hooks. It will help you visualize the finished product.

JUMP RINGS, HOOKS, AND CLASPS

The way a jewelry piece is attached to the wearer is crucial. Clasps, hooks, and jump rings are important elements to any jewelry design because, without them, we could all lose some beautiful jewelry. Although 21-gauge (0.71 mm) is an excellent gauge for just about any design, when making clasps, it's a good idea to use a fairly strong gauge of wire. If possible, try to stick to at least 20-gauge (0.80 mm) for any finding that works as a clasp in your finished jewelry design. Unless otherwise specified, 20-gauge (0.80 mm) is used for all the findings in this section.

PROJECT 1: BASIC JUMP RING

Jump rings are just simple wire circles but have a multitude of uses when it comes to making jewelry. The size of the jump rings you make depends on the diameter of the dowel, and the number of jump rings you make depends on the amount of wire you use.

MATERIALS

6" (15 cm) piece of wire
wooden dowel, pencil, or pen
jeweler's file
wire cutters

[A]

[B]

[C]

[D]

1. Begin by using your fingers to wrap your wire around your dowel (you can also use a pencil or pen for this) so that the wire is flush against it [A].

2. Slide the wire off the dowel so that you have a coil of wire.

3. Use a pair of flush-cut wire cutters to cut each coil one time to create a single ring [B].

4. Finally, use a jeweler's file to smooth the ends of the wire you just cut so that both ends of the jump ring are flat and can fit flush together [C and D].

jeweler's tip:

Try working with at least a 6" (15 cm) piece of wire when you make components or findings. Although you may need only an inch or two to make a hook or clasp, sometimes it can be much easier to work with a longer piece of wire, and you'll still have enough wire to make something else with the leftovers.

PROJECT 2: **BASIC HOOK**

This is one instance when it might be easier to work with a 6" (15 cm) piece of wire, though you don't need that much to complete this findings project successfully. It's really a matter of preference. Some jewelry makers find it easier to work with a longer piece of wire and some don't, but it's worth trying.

MATERIALS
1½" (3.75 cm) piece of wire
round-nose pliers
jeweler's file
wire cutters

1. After filing the ends of your wire, take your round-nosed pliers and make a loop or curl on one end of the wire [A].

2. Now, measuring approximately ½" (1.25 cm) from the end of the curl, grasp the wire with your round-nosed pliers using the middle part of the pliers' nose.

3. Holding your pliers with one hand, use your other hand to wrap the wire around the nose of your pliers to create a "hook" shape [B].

4. Using your round-nosed pliers, create a tiny curl on the end of the hook you created in the previous step [C].

[A]

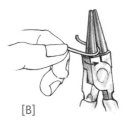

[B]

jeweler's tip:

Store your unused wire in an airtight container such as a large resealable plastic bag or plastic bowl with a lid. As sterling is exposed to oxygen, it oxidizes, and tarnish will build up on your wire. Label the outside of the bag or bowl with the wire gauge to help avoid confusion.

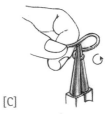

[C]

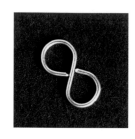

PROJECT 3: **BASIC EYE**

By using a little wire, you can fashion this basic eye design, which takes the form of a figure eight. The two loops on this piece combine to work as the second part of a clasp, which is made to team up with any number of hook-style clasps.

MATERIALS
1½" (3.75 cm) piece of wire
round-nose pliers
jeweler's file
wire cutters

1. Start by using a jeweler's file to smooth both ends of your wire.

2. Now use your round-nosed pliers to make a large loop on one end of the wire so that you have used up half of the piece of wire [A].

3. Do the same on the other end of the wire, but this time the loop should be facing in the other direction so that you make a figure eight (8) with the wire [B] .

[A]

[B]

jeweler's tip:

Before stringing a piece, consider how it will be worn. If it requires flexibility but also needs to be extra strong because of heavy beads, then beading wire is your best option. For a piece that needs to drape or has smalller beads (such as pearls or heishi besads), a softer stringing material, such as nylon or silk, is usually best.

BEAD AND WIRE TECHNIQUES

Once you learn to make your own findings, you also need to understand how to connect all the elements of your jewelry designs. This is when a number of different jewelry-making methods are required. Below are instructions for some of the most commonly used techniques for creating bead and wire jewelry.

WRAPPED LOOP

The wrapped loop technique is very useful for a large number of jewelry projects. You can use it to make earrings, add dangles to necklaces, or finish off a clasp for a bracelet. For this technique, you will need a pair of round-nosed pliers, wire cutters, flat-nosed pliers, a jeweler's file, and your choice of wire to create wrapped loops.

1. Start by using either the flat- or round-nosed pliers to bend the wire to a 90-degree angle so that you create an upside-down L shape [A and B].

2. Position the nose of your round-nosed pliers in the bend that you created in the previous step [C].

3. Use your fingers to wrap the wire around the nose of your pliers to form a loop [D].

4. While keeping the round-nosed pliers inside the loop, hold the loop against the nose of the pliers with one finger [E]. You should have your round-nosed pliers in one hand with one finger pressing the loop against the nose. (If you're right handed, then you'll probably want to use your left hand to hold the pliers and your pointer finger to hold the loop against the nose.)

5. Using your other hand (if you're right handed, the right hand), start to wrap the loose wire around the straight piece of wire that is directly under your loop. If the wire is soft, you can probably do this with your fingers. Otherwise, use bent-nosed (or flat-nosed, if you prefer) pliers to hold the loose wire and wrap [F].

continued

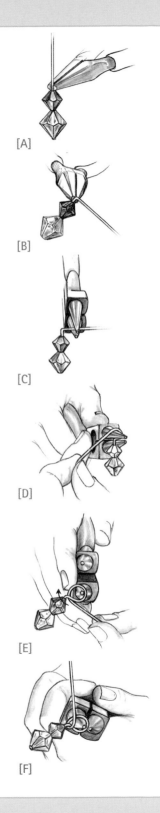

[A]

[B]

[C]

[D]

[E]

[F]

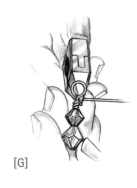

[G]

6. Continue to wrap as many times as you want. If necessary, trim off excess wire with wire cutters and file the ends smooth with a jeweler's file [G].

7. Use your bent-nosed pliers to press the wire-wrapped end flat, to make sure it doesn't scratch or poke the wearer.

8. If necessary, use your round-nosed pliers to straighten the loop.

SIMPLE LOOP

This technique is a simplified version of the wrapped loop technique and is useful for making earrings, dangles, pendants, and various other jewelry components. Although wrapping is more secure, if done properly, this simple loop technique can also be surprisingly strong. For this procedure, you will need a pair of round-nosed pliers, wire cutters, and a headpin. A headpin is being used for illustration purposes, but you can also use this technique with wire.

[A]

[B]

[C]

1. Use your round-nosed pliers to bend the headpin at a 90-degree angle [A].

2. Make sure the part of the headpin that's bent is about ½" long; if necessary, trim any excess with wire cutters.

3. Position the bent part of the headpin so that it's facing away from you.

4. Then, using round-nosed pliers, grasp the end of the bent headpin and make sure the middle part of the pliers' nose is holding the pin. After positioning your pliers correctly, curl the wire slowly toward you [B].

5. Because the first curl probably won't complete the entire loop, release and reposition your pliers on the loop that you've started.

6. Continue to curl it toward you until you've made a full circle [C].

CRIMP BEADS

A beaded piece of jewelry can be finished on the ends a number of different ways—using crimp beads to do this is one popular method. Some jewelry makers prefer the look of crimp beads to bead tips, but it's really a matter of personal preference. To use this method, you'll need a pair of crimping pliers, crimp beads (we recommend using tube-shaped crimp beads versus round crimp beads because they're much easier to work with), round-nosed pliers, wire cutters, and bead-ing wire. As with bead tips, you need to understand how to start and finish with crimp beads because there are a few minor differences.

1. Slide one crimp bead onto the end of a piece of beading wire, and loop the wire back through the crimp bead [A].

2. Position the crimp bead inside the second notch in the crimping pliers (the one closest to you when you're holding the pliers in your hand), and close the pliers around the bead. You should see the crimp bead now has a groove down the middle so that it curls [B].

3. Now, position the same crimp bead in the first notch in the pliers, and close the pliers around it so that you flatten the curl [C and D].

4. Use wire cutters to trim off all but about ¼" (5 mm) of excess beading wire.

5. Add your beads, making sure you slide the first bead over both pieces of wire on the end.

6. Once you've strung all your beads, you're ready to finish the other end. Slide a second crimp bead onto the end of your wire after the last bead strung.

7. Loop the wire back through the crimp bead as well as the last bead of the piece.

8. Insert the nose of your round-nosed pliers into the loop.

9. While holding your round-nosed pliers with one hand, gently pull the beading wire with your other hand so that you push the crimp bead up against the other beads. This will ensure that you don't have any extra slack in your beaded piece and that you also keep the end loop of your beading wire intact.

10. Repeat steps 2 and 3 above to close the crimp bead.

11. Finish by using wire cutters to trim off excess beading wire carefully.

[A]

[B]

[C]

[D]

BEAD TIPS

Bead tips are small metal findings used to start and finish off a beaded piece, such as a bracelet or necklace. Some people refer to them as clamshells because they have two cups that are open and look like a clam. Attached to the cup is a small hook that's attached to a clasp or a jump ring. You'll need to attach bead tips to the beginning and end of a piece. In addition to bead tips, you'll need your choice of cord (such as nylon or beading wire), flat-nosed pliers, scissors, jeweler's glue, and an awl or corsage pin.

[A]

1. To connect a bead tip to the beginning of a piece of beaded jewelry, start by tying at least two overhand knots, one on top of the other, at the end of your cord.

2. Slide the unknotted end of your cord down through the hole in the middle of the bead tip, and pull the cord so that the knot rests inside one of the shells [A].

3. Trim off the excess cord with scissors or wire cutters, and drop a small amount of jeweler's glue onto your knots.

4. Use flat-nosed pliers to close the two shells of the bead tip together [B and C].

5. String all of your beads.

6. When you're ready to finish off the piece with a bead tip, add another bead tip to the end by slipping the cord through the hole in the bead tip so that the open part of the bead tip (the shells) is facing away from the beads previously strung.

[B]

7. Tie a loose overhand knot with your cord, and insert an awl (or a corsage pin) into the knot.

8. Hold the cord with one hand and the awl with your other hand.

9. Use the awl to push the knot down into the bead tip, and pull tightly on the cord with your other hand.

10. Slip the awl out of the knot, and make another knot using this method, making sure that both knots fit inside one of the shells.

11. Trim off the excess cord, and drop a small amount of glue onto your knots.

[C]

12. Finish by using flat-nosed pliers to close the two shells of the bead tip together.

KNOTTING

Knotting between beads is a technique that many jewelry makers use when stringing high-end beads such as pearls. The knots between the beads allow for a nice draping effect when finished, and they also have a practical purpose. If a knotted necklace were to break, the beads will not roll off the strand. Also, the knots create a little space between the beads so they don't rub against each other. This is especially important for pearls or other soft beads. To knot between your beads, you need a beading awl (a corsage pin also works well); silk or nylon cord with an attached, twisted-wire needle; and your choice of beads.

1. Start by finishing one end of your cord in the technique you prefer. The bead tip technique works well for this.

2. Once your necklace is started, string your first bead onto the wire needle on the cord and push it down to the end of your necklace.

3. Tie a loose overhand knot [A].

4. Insert your beading awl through the loose knot [B].

5. Next, use one hand to push the awl and knot down toward the bead and hold onto the cord with your other hand until the awl and knot are flush up against the bead [C].

6. Keeping the knot up against the bead, carefully slip the end of your awl out of the knot and immediately use your fingers to push the knot against the bead.

7. Repeat this method for each bead that you wish to knot between.

[A]

[B]

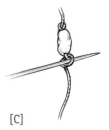

[C]

artist directory and index

Visit *1000 Jewelry Inspirations* at www.quarrybooks.com for a complete list of contributing jewelry designers.

Heather Mann
0232

Catherine Marché
0974

Andreia Cunha Martins
0363, 0694, 0696, 0744, 0918, 0921, 0925

Maureen Thomas Designs
0450, 0472, 0504, 0548, 0560

Ellene McClay
0395, 0734

McFarland Designs
0002, 0012, 0061, 0081, 0082, 0086, 0110, 0128,
0154, 0159, 0246, 0274, 0893, 0934, 0980

Kiara M. McNulty
0018, 0023, 0042, 0108, 0121, 0137, 0151, 0157,
0213, 0302, 0857

Melani Wilson Designs
0051, 0187, 0932

Mia Gofar Jewelry
0041, 0169, 0173, 0220, 0411, 0716, 0752, 0768,
0891

Micalla Jewelry and Designs, Camilla Jørgensen
0047, 0127, 0207, 0247, 0282

Miggipyn, Diane Wade
0619, 0621, 0622, 0665, 0668, 0762, 0839

Reuben Miller
0733, 0881

Modern Jewelry Designs
0007, 0322, 0390, 0956, 0976

Mona Song Designs
0130, 0198, 0249, 0313, 0880, 0906, 0911, 0913,
0930, 0955, 0981, 0995

Mood Swing
0073, 0186, 0295, 0397, 0611, 0613, 0644, 0647,
0650, 0679, 0682

Jane McGregor Hamilton Mormino
0350, 0403

Melissa Muir, Kelsi's Closet Jewelbox
0901, 0985

Sharon Muttoo
0011

N

Jessica Neaves
0286, 0870

Geraldine Newfry
0510, 0599

Vicky X. Nguyen
0868, 0885

Nicole Noelle
0004, 0005, 0124, 0125, 0167, 0268, 0269, 0270,
0272, 0273, 0275, 0288, 0289, 0290, 0291, 0292,
0297, 0309, 0312, 0684, 0729, 0739, 0960

Olga Noronha
0853, 0884, 0919, 0920, 0922, 0923, 0957, 0984,
0988

Vanda Noronha, paraphernalia.nu
0348

Halligan Norris
0338, 0339, 0340, 0341

Sally Nunnally
0095, 0214, 0257

O

Linda O'Brien
0347

Opie O'Brien
0412

Lauren E. Ochman, The Lola Collection
0357, 0359, 0414, 0416, 0486, 0487, 0488, 0489,
0490, 0491, 0492, 0493

Eni Oken
0927, 0965

P

Meream Pacayra
0745

Jenni Pagano
0114, 0126, 0142, 0156, 0753, 0793, 0794, 0849

Marcia Palmer
0448, 0452, 0453, 0457, 0469, 0498, 0512, 0513,
0514, 0516, 0568

Laurie E. Panariello
0876

Paper Flower Girl
0013, 0031, 0160, 0179, 0287, 0603, 0609, 0669,
0755, 0757, 0761, 0773, 0787, 0789, 0792, 0796,
0810, 0829, 0854, 0917, 0972

Janice Parsons
0248

Zuda Gay Pease, zudagay.etsy.com
0523, 0546, 0550, 0597

pequitobun
0607, 0629, 0632, 0633, 0634, 0635, 0636, 0637,
0638, 0651, 0652, 0653, 0663

Ana Pereira
0326, 0828, 0909, 0910, 0929

Jennifer Perkins
0639, 0640

Holly Piper-Smith, pollyhyper.etsy.com
0506, 0517, 0569, 0581, 0585

Debra Poth
0840, 0841, 0843

Tammy Powley
0030, 0032, 0033, 0056, 0066, 0118, 0140, 0164,
0165, 0168, 0177, 0218, 0222, 0223, 0225, 0226,
0227, 0228, 0238, 0241, 0244, 0245, 0253, 0259,
0263, 0278, 0284, 0285, 0327, 0905, 0970, 0990

Enrica Prazzoli
0735, 0748

Precious Meshes, Emily Conroy
0210, 0899, 0904, 0935, 0938

Pretty•Fun
0366, 0383, 0409

Peggy Prielozny
0065, 0833

Rachel Pryden
0459

R

Toni M. Ransfield
0598

relishdress
0293, 0683, 0698, 0770, 0797, 0802, 0807, 0818,
0824, 0860, 0867, 0914

Rickie Voges Design
0040, 0045, 0062, 0068, 0122, 0146, 0242, 0265

Rocca Designs, Carolina Estrada
0192, 0255, 0896, 0900

Rosebonbon
0427, 0432, 0671, 0677, 0754, 0783, 0819

resources

USA

Addicted To Rubber Stamps
800-913-2877
www.addictedtorubberstamps.com
Rubber stamping supplies

Artgems Inc.
480-545-6009
www.artgemsinc.com
Bead, findings, and related jewelry supplies

Auntie's Beads
866-262-3237
www.auntiesbeads.com
Beads and general jewelry-making supplies

Beadalon
866-423-2325
www.beadalon.com
Beading wire, memory wire, and general jewelry supplies

The Bead Shop
650-383-3408
www.beadshopboutique.com
Beads, jewelry-making supplies, kits, DVDs, and CDs

The Bead Warehouse
301-565-0487
www.thebeadwarehouse.com
Stone beads and general jewelry-making supplies

B'Sue Boutiques
www.bsueboutiques.com
General beading supplies, vintage and vintage-inspired findings, and metal stampings

CGM
800-426-5246
www.cgmfindings.com
Wholesale wire, metal beads, and findings

Earthstone
800-747-8088
www.earthstone.com
Pearls and gemstones

Environmental Technologies Inc.
707-443-9323
www.eti-usa.com
Consumer and industrial products for resin casting

Fire Mountain Gems and Beads
800-423-2319
www.firemountaingems.com
General jewelry-making supplies, books, and displays

Gemshow-Online Jewelry Supply
877-805-7440
www.gemshow-online.com
Crystals, metal beads, and findings

Golden Sea Advance Inc.
626-291-2277
www.goldenseaadv.com
Pearls and gemstones

A Grain of Sand
704-660-3125
www.agrainofsand.com
Vintage and contemporary beads and findings

Halstead Bead, Inc.
800-528-0535
www.halsteadbead.com
Findings, metal, crystal, and other related jewelry-related supplies

HHH Enterprises
800-777-0218
www.hhhenterprises.com
General jewelry-making supplies

Land of Odds
615-292-0610
www.landofodds.com
General jewelry-making supplies and seed beads

Monsterslayer, Inc.
505-598-5322
www.monsterslayer.com
Metal findings, wire, and beads

Nina Designs
800-336-6462
www.ninadesigns.com
Clasps, Bali silver, and findings

Ornametea
919-834-6260
www.ornamentea.com
Mixed-media jewelry, fiber beads, and related supplies

Out on a Whim
800-232-3111
www.whimbeads.com
Seed beads, crystals, and findings

Rings & Things
800-366-2156
www.rings-things.com
Wholesale jewelry-making supplies

Rio Grande
800-545-6566
www.riogrande.com
Equipment, beads, metal, and related jewelry supplies

Scrapbooking Supplies R Us
800-352-1980
www.scrapbookingsuppliesrus.com
Embellishments, albums, and related scrapbooking accessories

Scrapbooking Warehouse
831-768-1810
www.scrapbooking-warehouse.com
Scrapbooking and rubber stamp products

Shipwreck Beads
360-754-2323
www.shipwreckbeads.com
General jewelry-making supplies

Soft Flex Company
866-925-3539
www.softflextm.com
Soft Flex beading wire and general jewelry-making supplies

South Pacific Wholesale Co.
800-338-2162
www.beading.com
Stone beads and general jewelry-making supplies

Stampington & Company
877-782-6737
www.stampington.com
Rubber stamp and paper arts products

Stuller, Inc.
800-877-7777
www.stuller.com
Large catalog of jewelry-related supplies in all categories

TAJ Company
800-325-0825
www.tajcompany.com
Pearls and gemstones

AUSTRALIA

Aussie Scrapbooking Studio
08 8288 1141
www.scrapbookingstudio.com
General scrapbooking supplies

The Bead Company
08 9244 2424
www.beadco.com.au
Beads and general jewelry-making supplies

Katie's Treasures
02 4968 9485
www.katiestreasures.com.au
Pearls, beads, and related jewelry-related supplies

Spacetrader Beads
03 9534 6867
www.spacetrader.com.au
Pearls, beads, and related jewelry-related supplies

CANADA

BeadFX
877-473-2323
www.beadfx.com
Pearls, beads, crystal, and findings

Canadian Beading Supply
800-291-6668
www.canbead.com
Large catalog of jewelry-related supplies

The House of Orange
250-483-1468
toll free in US and Canada: 866-401-9174
www.houseoforange.biz
Beads, crystal, and general jewelry-related supplies

UNITED KINGDOM

African Trade Beads
www.africantradebeads.com
Czech, seed, and various imported beads

Beadgems
0845 123 2743
www.beadgems.com
Pearls, beads, crystal, and findings

Beads Unlimited
0127 374 0777
www.beadsunlimited.co.uk
Beads and related supplies

Beadworks
020 8553 3240
www.beadworks.co.uk
General beading supplies

Gem Craft
0161 477 0435
www.gemcraft.co.uk
Gem and mineral supplier

Hobbycraft
Stores throughout the United Kingdom
0120 259 6100
www.hobbycraft.co.uk
Bead shop and jewelry-making supplier

Kernowcraft Rocks & Gems Ltd
01872 573888
www.kernowcraft.com
Pearls, beads, and jewelry-related supplies